Cambridge Latin Course

Book III

Student Study Book
Answer Key

FOURTH EDITION

CAMBRIDGE
UNIVERSITY PRESS

University Printing House, Cambridge CB2 8BS, United Kingdom

Cambridge University Press is part of the University of Cambridge.

It furthers the University's mission by disseminating knowledge in the pursuit of education, learning and research at the highest international levels of excellence.

Information on this title: education.cambridge.org

© University of Cambridge School Classics Project 2004, 2007

First published by the University of Cambridge School Classics Project
as *Independent Learning Answer Book III* 2004
Fourth edition 2007
7th printing 2014

Printed in the United Kingdom by Printondemand-worldwide, Peterborough

A catalogue record for this publication is available from the British Library

ISBN 978-0-521-68596-2 Paperback

Cambridge University Press has no responsibility for the persistence or accuracy of URLs for external or third-party internet websites referred to in this publication, and does not guarantee that any content on such websites is, or will remain, accurate or appropriate. Information regarding prices, travel timetables, and other factual information given in this work is correct at the time of first printing but Cambridge University Press does not guarantee the accuracy of such information thereafter.

Stage 21 Aquae Sūlis

Model sentences

Translation pp. 2–4

1   In the town of Aquae Sulis / Bath were working many craftsmen/workmen, who were building very large baths. A Roman architect was inspecting the craftsmen.

2   The first craftsman was making a statue of the goddess Sulis. The architect praised the craftsman, because he was skilful and was working hard. The craftsman, having been praised by the architect, was very happy.

3   The second craftsman was putting a wall round the spring. The architect urged on the craftsman, because he was tired and was working slowly. The craftsman, having been urged on by the architect, took the criticism (*literally* the thing) badly. However, he said nothing, because he was afraid of the architect.

4   The third craftsman was carrying water to the bath from the sacred spring. The architect cursed the craftsman, because he was lazy and was doing very little work. The craftsman, having been cursed by the architect, replied insolently.

5   When the architect heard the insolent words of the craftsman, he summoned his slaves. The slaves, having been summoned by the architect, seized the craftsman and threw him into the bath.

6   'You have a dirty tongue', said the architect, laughing. 'It is / would be better for you to drink the sacred water.'

Questions SSB pp. 1–2

Sentences 1

a   The craftsmen were building very big baths.

b   The architect was inspecting the craftsmen.

c   He was wearing a toga.

Sentences 2

a   The first craftsman was making a statue of the goddess Sulis.

b   The architect praised him because he was skilful and was working hard.

c   *The craftsman, having been **praised** by the architect, was very happy.*

Sentences 3

a   The second craftsman was putting a wall round the spring.

b   The architect urged him on because he was tired and was working slowly.

c   *The craftsman, **having been** urged on by the architect, took the criticism (lit. the thing) badly.*

d   He did not reply because he was afraid of the architect.

Sentences 4

a   The third workman was carrying water to the bath from the sacred spring.

b   The architect cursed the workman because he was lazy and was doing very little work.

c   *The workman, **having been cursed** by the architect, replied insolently.*

Sentences 5

a   The architect summoned his slaves when he heard the workman's rude words.

b   They seized the workman and threw him into the bath.

c   **(servī) ab architectō arcessītī** *(the slaves) having been summoned by the architect.*

Sentences 6

a   The architect said that the workman had a dirty tongue (referring to his rudeness), which therefore needed to be washed by drinking the sacred water.

b   **cachinnāns** *cackling, roaring with laughter.*

The translations of **laudātus**, **incitātus**, etc. *having been praised, having been urged on*, etc., sound very unnatural. There are better ways of translating these new forms. However, it will help your understanding of the forms, if initially you keep to this particular kind of translation.

fōns sacer   p. 5 SSB p. 3

1   At Salvius' house, with Salvius.

2   To Cogidubnus' palace.

3   Quintus told him (Cogidubnus) many things about the city of Alexandria, because the king always wanted to hear something new.

4   When spring was approaching.

5   *Many doctors,* **having been summoned** *to the palace, sought a cure for the illness.*

6   **ingravēscēbat tamen morbus.** *However, the illness was growing worse.*

7   He thought Quintus was a wise man.

8   'Should I go to the sacred spring?' / He asked Quintus whether he should go to the sacred spring.

9   Many invalids, who had drunk the water from that spring, had afterwards recovered.

10   The very big baths and the temple of the goddess Sulis.

11   a   A Roman architect, having been sent by me.

    b   The temple of the goddess Sulis, having been built by my workmen/craftsmen.

12   He hoped that the goddess could perhaps cure him.

13   He said Salvius was a man of great cleverness / a very clever man.

14   Salvius thought it would be better for Cogidubnus to make a will.

15   Your answers may reflect the following thoughts and feelings:

Salvius: sceptical about the power of the sacred spring, thinking about what would happen if the king were to die, maybe even wishing him to die.

Cogidubnus: ill and anxious about what he should do, worried about how serious his illness was, hoping the goddess would cure him.

Quintus: concerned about his friend, wondering what advice he should give, trying to reassure him.

Lūcius Marcius Memor

Questions   p. 7

                                                  Marks

1   Aquae Sulis was only a small town but it had a very large set of baths.   1

2   **obēsus** *fat*; **ignāvus** *lazy.*   2

3   Late; the words **quamquam** *although* and **iam** *already* emphasise this / Roman hours went from dawn to dusk, so that the third hour was well into the morning; Romans generally rose very early.   1

4   **ēbrius. rūrsus** (meaning *again*) suggests that Memor was often drunk.   2

5   Memor ordered Cephalus to bring him more wine and then go away.   2
He thought Cephalus could deal with the business himself.   1

6   Cephalus was stressing that only the procurator could issue orders / He was trying to flatter Memor by emphasising his position / He was trying to impress upon him his duty as procurator.   1

7   Anger/laughter/disbelief. Memor did no work and could not possibly feel tired.   2

8   Memor has not been able to cultivate powerful men, since there were few of them in Britain.   2

9   Memor ordered Cephalus to send everyone away. He told him not to annoy him again. Memor then immediately fell asleep.   3

10   **territus, invītus.**   2

11   Cephalus found a great number of men shouting loudly and cursing the absent Memor.   2

12 *Two of:*

> **multī servī**; **multī fabrī**: stressing the number of people waiting.
> **exspectant**; **(tē) exspectat**; **(tē) exspectant**: emphasising waiting.
> **tē**; **tē**: emphasising that it is Memor whom people are waiting for.
> **adsunt**; **adsunt**: again stressing the idea that people are present and that they need attention urgently.
> **rem … administrāre**; **rem administrāre**: emphasising that Cephalus cannot (**nōn possum**) sort out the matter, but that Memor himself (**ipse**) should be dealing with it.   2 + 2
> *1 mark for picking out each pair of repeated words or phrases; 1 mark for each explanation.*

———

TOTAL 25

Further work SSB p. 4

Line	Latin	English	Description
1	maximae	very large	superlative
2	nōtissimus	very famous	superlative
5	excitāre	to wake up	infinitive
7	dormiēns	sleeping	present participle
9	surge!	get up!	imperative
11	abī!	go away!	imperative
12	surgere	to get up	infinitive

Line	Description	Translation	Person(s)
21–2	quam fessus sum!	How tired I am!	Memor
25	paucī (twice)	few	powerful men, famous men
30	territus	terrified	Cephalus
31	vehementer clāmantēs	shouting loudly	very many men

General question SSB p. 4

Here are some impressions of the characters of Memor and Cephalus. You may have other views.

Memor

He is lazy, more interested in heavy drinking than his responsibilities as manager of the baths. He complains about his workload and life in Britain. He is depressed because he cannot see any way of advancing his career because there are no influential patrons in Britain for him to cultivate. It never occurs to him to do any work himself. He delegates his work to Cephalus, yet shows no appreciation of his freedman's efforts. He is a thoroughly selfish person, out to improve his own position but with no feeling for his job or for other people.

Cephalus

An efficient assistant to Memor, he knows what his master should be doing, is willing to help him, but has the sense to realise that he cannot take over all Memor's work as manager of the baths. However, his fear of Memor's anger drives him to do things he knows are unwise, like dismissing all those waiting to see Memor in the baths.

Aquae Sulis and its baths

pp. 14–20 SSB pp. 5–6

1   Aquae Sulis lies in the valley of the river Avon. See the map on p. 139.

2   **a** and **b.** These are open questions, with scope for a variety of answers. Here are some points which you may like to think about if you have not already done so.

   a   *What would have impressed Rusonia Aventina / Julius Vitalis about their visit to Bath?* Although they were both familiar with Roman life and buildings, they would probably have been struck by the great size of the baths, the phenomenon of the hot springs and the new temple with its strange pediment (see pp. 18 and 40). The crowds of visitors and no doubt stories about miraculous cures would have given Bath a very special atmosphere.

   Why did Rusonia and Julius come to Bath? The obvious answer is that they were both ill and hoping (in vain) for a cure. Rusonia, who may have travelled the long distance from Metz in eastern France, may have been further weakened by her long journey. However, they may have been visiting Bath as tourists. Julius may have been on leave from the fortress at Chester and have come to Bath with a group of fellow soldiers to have a good time. His death and that of Rusonia may have been due to illness, an accident or some violent incident.

   Who put up their tombstones? Julius' tombstone was probably ordered and paid for by his legion's burial club, while that of Rusonia may have been erected by her family who were perhaps travelling with her.

   b   *The anti-Roman Celt.* You are appalled by the vast new developments at Bath and the commercialisation of the sacred spring. You regret the loss of your traditional way of life and worship, and your closeness to nature. You resent paying taxes to the Romans.

   The pro-Roman Celt. You have never seen such magnificent buildings before; in fact, you have never seen stone buildings, except standing stones erected by your ancestors long ago. You are proud that your goddess Sulis and her healing powers have become so famous and that so many visit her sacred spring. You are relieved that the Roman conquerors have respected your goddess and have identified her with one of theirs, Minerva, and have built a great temple in her honour. Despite the taxes you have to pay, you hope the Romans will bring added prosperity to your land.

4   **a**   Large pewter **jugs**.

   b   Pewter dish.

   c   Silver saucepan. The handle shown on p. 1 was attached to a saucepan like this.

   d   Bronze saucepan. The decoration was originally filled with enamel.

   e   Pewter **saucepans**. These are inscribed with the words **SULI MINERVAE** and **DSM (DEAE SULI MINERVAE)**, meaning *for (the goddess) Sulis Minerva.* Probably used in temple rituals.

   f   Bone handle of clasp knife.

   g   Curse tablet. This will be explained in the next Stage.

   h   Bronze washer from small military catapult, similar in strength to medieval crossbow.

   i   Ivory carving of a pair of breasts, perhaps given to the goddess in gratitude for healing.

   j   **Ear-ring**.

   k   Sheet of bronze with cut-out pattern, perhaps part of priest's ritual dress.

   l   **Heap of coins**. 10,000–20,000 coins were found in the spring, of which four gold coins were valuable; many were silver, and the rest bronze and brass of low value.

m Two pewter **bowls** and a pewter **plate**.

n Tin mask, 33 cm high, previously attached to wooden backing, used in the temple ritual.

o **Carved gemstones**. They were probably thrown in all together in a bag.

p Pewter inkpot.

senātor advenit

Translation of cartoon story SSB p. 6

1   Cephalus returned from the baths. He again entered the bedroom and woke up the sleeping Memor.

Memor: *Why are you preventing me from sleeping? You are more stupid than a donkey.*

Cephalus: *I want to tell you something new. I have caught sight of a senator approaching the baths.*

2   **Memor**: *Who is that senator? Where has he come from? I don't want to see a senator.*

Cephalus: *It would be better for you to see this senator. For he is Gaius Salvius.*

Memor: *Surely not Gaius Salvius Liberalis? I don't believe you.*

3   Cephalus, however, easily persuaded him, because Salvius was already riding into the courtyard of the baths.

Memor: *Bring me my toga! Bring me my shoes! Where are my decorations? Call the slaves! How unlucky I am! Salvius is coming here, a man of the highest authority (or a very important man), whom I especially want to cultivate.*

4   Memor very quickly put on his toga and shoes. Cephalus handed him his decorations, hastily pulled out of a cupboard.

The soothsayer kept on blaming the innocent freedman, the freedman (kept on blaming) Salvius.

Questions SSB p. 7

1   cūr prohibēs mē dormīre?
Why are you preventing me from sleeping?
quis est ille senātor?
Who is that senator?
unde vēnit?
Where has he come from?
num Gāius Salvius Līberālis?
Surely not Gaius Salvius Liberalis?
ōrnāmenta mea ubi sunt?
Where are my decorations?

2   stultior es **quam** asinus.
*You are more stupid **than** a donkey.*
quam īnfēlīx sum!
How unlucky I am!

3 **a** dormientem *sleeping*
     noun: **Memorem**

   b appropinquantem *approaching*
     noun: **senātōrem**

Translation of the complete story p. 8

Cephalus returned from the baths. He again entered the bedroom and woke up the sleeping Memor. As soon as Memor saw Cephalus, he shouted angrily,

'Why are you preventing me from sleeping? Why don't you obey me? You are more stupid than a donkey.'

'But, master', said Cephalus, 'I want to tell you something new. After I left here, I carried out the orders, which you gave me. However, when I was sending away the invalids and the workmen, I caught sight of a senator approaching the baths.'

Memor, very annoyed, said,

'Who is that senator? Where has he come from? I don't want to see a senator.'

'It would be better for you to see this senator', said Cephalus. 'For he is Gaius Salvius.'

'Surely not Gaius Salvius Liberalis?' cried Memor. 'I don't believe you.'

Cephalus, however, easily persuaded him, because Salvius was already riding into the courtyard of the baths.

Memor, terrified, at once shouted,

'Bring me my toga! Bring my shoes! Where are my decorations? Call the slaves! How unlucky I am! Salvius is coming here, a man of the highest authority (*or* a very important man), whom I especially want to cultivate.'

Memor very quickly put on his toga and shoes. Cephalus handed him his decorations, hastily pulled out of a cupboard. The soothsayer kept on blaming the innocent freedman, the freedman (kept on blaming) Salvius.

About the language: perfect passive participles p. 9   SSB p. 8

1 **quaerentēs** describes **servī** and is therefore nominative plural. **sedentem** describes **mātrem** and is therefore accusative singular.

2 **aedificātae** describes **thermae**.

4 a The slave, having been beaten by the master, fled from the town.

  b The messengers, having been summoned by the king, told a terrible story.

  c The slave-girl, having been praised by Quintus, was very happy.

  d The temple, having been built by skilled workmen, was splendid.

  e The soldiers, having been wounded by the enemy, wanted to visit the baths.

  f The wife, having been annoyed by her husband, left the house.

	Perfect passive participle	Noun	Singular or plural
a	verberātus	servus	singular
b	arcessītī	nūntiī	plural
c	laudāta	ancilla	singular
d	aedificātum	templum	singular
e	vulnerātī	mīlitēs	plural
f	vexāta	uxor	singular

Further exercise

1 The craftsman, having been told off by the architect, replied rudely.

When the craftsman was told off by the architect, he replied rudely.

2 Many doctors, having been summoned to the palace, looked for a cure for the disease.

When many doctors were summoned to the palace, they looked for a cure for the disease.

3 Memor, having at last been woken up by his freedman, opened one eye.

Memor, woken up at last by his freedman, opened one eye.

4 Cephalus, having been terrified by his angry master, reluctantly went out.

Cephalus, terrified by his angry master, reluctantly went out.

5 There were soldiers present, having been wounded by the enemy.

There were soldiers present, who had been wounded by the enemy.

These are some suggestions: other translations are possible too.

Memor rem suscipit I

Translation pp. 10–11   SSB pp. 8–9

Salvius and Memor, walking alone in the garden, are having a serious conversation.

Salvius: Lucius Marcius Memor, you are a man of the highest intelligence. I want you to undertake an important task.

Memor: **I should like to undertake such a task, but I am very busy. Invalids and priests are waiting for me. The architect and workmen are annoying me. But what do you want me to do?**

Salvius: Tiberius Claudius Cogidubnus, king of the Regnenses, has recently arrived here. Cogidubnus, who has fallen seriously ill (*lit.* has fallen into a serious illness), wants to drink the water from the sacred spring.

Memor: **It is difficult for me to help you, my dear senator. Cogidubnus is eighty years old (*lit.* a man of eighty years). It is difficult for the goddess Sulis to cure Cogidubnus.**

Salvius: I don't want you to make Cogidubnus well. I want you to do the opposite.

Memor: **What do you mean? Surely you do not want Cogidubnus' death?**

Salvius: Yes! What's more, although you are so busy, I want you to carry out this job yourself.

Memor: **You want me to kill the king? I do not want to do a thing of this kind. For Cogidubnus is a very famous man, honoured by the Roman people.**

Salvius: You are a very shrewd man (*lit.* a man of the greatest shrewdness). You can carry out this mission. Not only I, but also the emperor, wants this. For Cogidubnus has often annoyed the Romans. The emperor trusts me, not Cogidubnus. The emperor promises you an appropriate reward. Surely you don't want to refuse the reward promised by the emperor?

Memor: **How can I do the job?**

Salvius: I don't know. I say only this to you: the emperor awaits the death of Cogidubnus.

Memor: **Oh dear! I have never done anything more difficult.**

Salvius: Life, my dear Memor, is full of difficult things.
(*Salvius goes out.*)

Questions SSB pp. 9–10

1 Salvius and Memor are walking in the garden alone, so that there is no risk that they will be overheard.

2 Salvius calls Memor 'a man of the highest intelligence' to flatter him in the hope that he will agree to murder Cogidubnus.

3 Memor says he would like to undertake the important piece of work for Salvius, but he is lying, as we know he is extremely lazy. His excuse is that he is extremely busy with managing the baths, but again we know that he neglects his duties and leads a life of idleness. However, he is curious to know what Salvius' job is, just in case it is profitable for him.

4 By giving the details Memor is emphasising how busy he is.

5 The tone may change twice: first, after **velim**, where Memor is pretending that he would really like Salvius' job, but then sounds regretful and harassed because he is so busy;

second, after **fabrī**, where curiosity gets the better of him and he asks Salvius what he wants him to do.

6 Memor thinks Salvius is asking him to help cure Cogidubnus. This is clear when he replies that it is difficult for him to help Salvius. Cogidubnus is eighty, and the goddess would find it difficult to cure Cogidubnus.

7 Memor is reluctant because Cogidubnus is very famous and has been honoured by the Roman people.

8 No. Cogidubnus was a great help to the Romans in the invasion and supports their rule now.

9 Memor finally agrees to carry out the plan because Salvius says that it is the emperor's wish and that the emperor is promising him an appropriate reward, an offer that he surely cannot refuse.

10 Salvius' response is entirely negative. He says he does not know how Memor can effect the murder, but that the emperor expects it – a veiled threat. When Memor complains about the difficulty of the task, Salvius merely utters the unhelpful remark that life is full of difficulties.

Further work SSB p. 10

1 I want you to undertake an important task.
Imperfect: **volēbam**. *I wanted you to undertake an important task.*

2 What do you want me to do?
Imperfect: **volēbās**. *What did you want me to do?*

3 I do not want to do this.
Imperfect: **nōlēbam**. *I did not want to do this.*

4 Cogidubnus is a very famous man.
Imperfect: **erat**. *Cogidubnus was a very famous man.*

5 I cannot / am not able to kill the king.
Imperfect: **poteram**. *I could not / was not able to kill the king.*

6 Surely we can / are able to help the emperor?
Imperfect: **poterāmus**. *Surely we could / were able to help the emperor?*

Memor rem suscipit II

Translation p. 11

Memor: Cephalus! Cephalus! *(The freedman, called by Memor, enters quickly. He is carrying a cup of wine.)* Why are you offering me wine? I'm not looking for wine, but advice. I order you to give me advice as quickly as possible. King Cogidubnus has come here, seeking a cure for his illness. The emperor, who has often been annoyed by Cogidubnus, now wants his death. The emperor himself orders me to bring this about. How difficult it is!

Cephalus: No, it is easy! I have a poisoned cup, which was once given to me by an Egyptian robber. The poison, hidden in the cup, can destroy life very quickly.

Memor: The plan, which you are proposing to me, is dangerous. I am afraid to give poison to Cogidubnus.

Cephalus: There is no danger. The king, whenever he gets out of the bath, is accustomed to go to the goddess' spring. Then it is necessary for a slave to stand near the goddess' spring and to offer the cup to the king.

Memor: *(delighted)* It is an excellent plan. I do not, however, trust any slaves. But I trust you, Cephalus. I order you to offer the cup to Cogidubnus yourself.

Cephalus: Alas! You are imposing a very difficult task upon me.

Memor: Life, my dear Cephalus, is full of difficult things.

Questions SSB pp. 10–11

1 *Memor*: Initially he panics about the difficulty of contriving Cogidubnus' death and is desperate for Cephalus to help him out; then he worries about the danger of poisoning Cogidubnus (what if he were caught?); finally he is delighted when Cephalus not only provides him with an excellent plan but is the perfect candidate to carry it out. His final line would be delivered with a smug flourish as he has managed to pass on to Cephalus the problem given him by Salvius. He must enjoy repeating Salvius' very words. See the final line of **Memor rem suscipit I**.

Cephalus: At first he is fed up with Memor's whingeing and eager to propose his clever solution; then he is dismissive of Memor's worry about the danger and keen to counter his stupidity with the ease of his plan; finally he is annoyed at having opened the way for Memor to make him carry out the murder.

2 **a** cūr **mihi** vīnum offers?
*Why do you offer **me** wine?*
Or, *Why do you offer wine **to me**?*
lībertus **dominō** vīnum offert.
*The freedman offers wine **to his master**.*
Or, *The freedman offers **his master** wine.*

b cōnsilium, quod **mihi** prōpōnis, perīculōsum est.
*The plan which you are proposing **to me** is dangerous.*
Cephalus **haruspicī** cōnsilium callidum prōpōnit.
*Cephalus proposes a clever plan **to the soothsayer**.*

c **nūllīs servīs** cōnfīdō.
*I do not trust **any slaves** (lit. I trust no slaves).*
Memor **lībertō** cōnfīdit.
*Memor trusts **his freedman**.*

d iubeō tē ipsum **Cogidubnō** pōculum praebēre.
*I order you yourself to offer **Cogidubnus** the cup.*
Or, *I order you yourself to offer the cup **to Cogidubnus**.*
necesse est **Cephalō** venēnum **rēgī** dare.
*It is necessary **for Cephalus** to give the poison **to the king**.*
Or, *It is necessary **for Cephalus** to give **the king** the poison.*

3	Line	Perfect passive participle	Latin noun described	Translated sentence
	1	vocātus	lībertus	The freedman, called by Memor, enters quickly.
	6	vexātus	Imperātor	The emperor, who has often been annoyed by Cogidubnus, now wants his death.
	10	datum	pōculum	I have a poisoned cup, which was once given to me by an Egyptian robber.
	11	cēlātum	venēnum	The poison, hidden in the cup, can destroy life very quickly.
	17	dēlectātus	Memor	Delighted.

Word patterns: adjectives and adverbs p. 12

3

adjectives		*adverbs*	
cautus	*cautious*	cautē	***cautiously***
superbus	*proud*	**superbē**	*proudly*
crūdēlissimus	*very cruel*	**crūdēlissimē**	***very cruelly***

4

adjectives		*adverbs*	
gravissimus	*very serious*	intentē	*closely*
callidus	*clever*	tacitē	*quietly*
ignāvus	*lazy*	firmē	*firmly*
dīligentissimus	*very careful*	saevissimē	*very savagely*

5
- **a** dūrissimus
- **b** probē
- **c** līberālissimē
- **d** cautus, lentē

Practising the language

p. 13 SSB pp. 11–12

1
- **a** omnēs aegrōtī **fontem** vīsitāre volēbant.
  All the invalids wanted to visit the spring.
  fontem: accusative singular
- **b** plūrimī servī in fundō **dominī** labōrābant.
  Very many slaves were working on their master's farm.
  dominī: genitive singular
- **c** 'fortasse **dea** morbum meum sānāre potest', inquit rēx.
  'Perhaps the goddess can cure my disease',
  said the king.
  dea: nominative singular
- **d** **prīncipēs** Cogidubnum laudāvērunt, quod līberālis et sapiēns erat.
  The chieftains praised Cogidubnus, because he was generous and wise.
  prīncipēs: nominative plural

e   mercātor, postquam **dēnāriōs** accēpit, ē forō discessit.
    After the merchant received the denarii (or money), he left the forum.
    dēnāriōs: accusative plural

f   senex, quī in Aegyptō diū habitāverat, magnum numerum **statuārum** comparāverat.
    The old man, who had lived in Egypt for a long time, had obtained a large number of statues.
    statuārum: genitive plural

2   a   sacerdōtēs statuam architectō ostendērunt.

    b   rēx medicum perītum laudāvit.

    c   amīcus mīlitum templum vīsitābat.

    d   clāmōrēs aegrōtōrum haruspicem vexāverant.

    e   pecūniam dominī agricolīs trādidimus.

3   a   tū ipse hanc rem administrāre **dēbēs**.
        You yourself must / ought to manage this task.

    b   cūr mē vituperās? heri per tōtum diem **labōrāvī**.
        Why are you blaming me? Yesterday I worked through the whole day.

    c   ego, quod fontem sacrum vidēre **cupiēbam**, iter ad oppidum Aquās Sūlis fēcī.
        Because I wanted to see the sacred spring, I made the journey to the town of Bath.

    d   lībertus, quī senātōrem **cōnspexerat**, in cubiculum haruspicis ruit.
        The freedman, who had caught sight of the senator, rushed into the soothsayer's bedroom.

    e   ē lectō surrēxī, quod dormīre nōn **poteram**.
        I got out of bed, because I could not sleep.

    f   in hāc vīllā **habitat** Memor, haruspex nōtissimus.
        In this villa lives Memor, a very well-known soothsayer.

Vocabulary   p. 168

4   amāvī *I (have) loved*; laudātus *having been praised*; monitus *having been warned/advised*; terrēre *to frighten*; ductus *having been led*; neglēxī *I (have) neglected/ignored*; clausus *having been shut/closed*; mīsī *I (have) sent*; fundere *to pour*; fūdī *I (have) poured*; relinquō *I leave / am leaving*; relictus *having been left*; custōdītus *having been guarded*; impedīvī *I (have) hindered*.

Vocabulary checklist 21   SSB p. 12

1   The job of an *adjutant* is to help the commanding officer (from **adiuvō**).

2   *Annuals* last just for a year; *perennials* last for many (from **annus**).

3   Examples include: *circumnavigate*; *circumference*; *circumspect*; *circumlocution*; *circumscribe*; *circumflex*; *circumstance*; *circumvent*. There are many more possibilities.

4   If you are *efficient*, you accomplish a lot; you get things done quickly and well.

5   He regarded the crime as being very serious (from **gravis**). **gravis** can also mean *heavy*, hence *gravity* is also used to mean the pull of objects towards the earth.

6   A *morbid* interest would be a fascination with hospital TV programmes bordering on the obsessive and therefore like an illness (from **morbus**).

7   The sign is often called the *plus* sign. The Latin word is the same: **plūs**, meaning *more*.

8   **pretium** means *price*; **pretiōsus** means *expensive, precious* or *pricey*, i.e. costing a high price.

9   **homō sapiēns** (lit. *wise man*) is the biological name for a human being.

10 *conceal*: **cēlō**. To conceal something means to hide it.
    endure: **dūrus**. To endure something means to be hard enough to withstand it (e.g. a hard object will endure the ravages of time; a tough person will endure tough punishment).
    replenish: **plēnus**. To replenish something means to fill it up again.

Language test SSB pp. 12–13

1   a   The craftsmen, having been sent by the
        king, built the baths and temple.
        Or, The craftsmen, sent by the king, built
        the baths and temple.

    b   The baths, having been built by the
        craftsmen, were very big.
        Or, The baths, built by the craftsmen,
        were very big.

    c   Cephalus, having been ordered by
        Memor, brought in some wine.
        Or, When he was ordered by Memor,
        Cephalus brought in some wine.

    d   The craftsman, having been thrown into
        the bath, cursed the architect.
        Or, The craftsman, who had been thrown
        into the bath, cursed the architect.

    e   Salvius, having been asked by
        Cogidubnus, gave his advice.
        Or, When he was asked by Cogidubnus,
        Salvius gave his advice.

    f   Memor did not want to refuse the reward
        having been promised by the emperor.
        Or, Memor did not want to refuse the
        reward promised by the emperor.

Noun	Participle	Singular/plural
a fabrī	missī	plural
b thermae	aedificātae	plural
c Cephalus	iussus	singular
d faber	dēiectus	singular
e Salvius	rogātus	singular
f praemium	prōmissum	singular

2   a   Quintus told the king many things about
        the city of Alexandria.
        rēgī: dative singular (*lit.* told to the king)

    b   Memor, who had now been asleep for
        many hours, opened one eye.
        oculum: accusative singular

    c   Many craftsmen (and) several merchants
        were waiting for Memor.
        mercātōrēs: nominative plural

    d   Cephalus often gave the master's
        instructions to the slaves.
        servīs: dative plural

    e   Memor did not believe the freedman's
        words.
        lībertī: genitive singular

    f   'Oh dear!' said Memor. 'This town is full
        of very troublesome men.'
        hominum: genitive plural

Revision

Verbs SSB p. 13

1
-nt	they
-ō	I
-mus	we
-tis	you (pl.)
-istis	you (pl.)
-t	s/he, it
-m	I
-istī	you (s.)
-ī	I
-s	you (s.)

2   a   I help; I (have) helped; you (s.) (have)
        helped.

    b   they hide; we hide; we have hidden, we
        hid.

    c   you (pl.) accomplish; you (pl.)
        (have) accomplished; you (pl.) had
        accomplished.

    d   you (s.) were ordering; you (s.) (have)
        ordered; I had ordered.

Adjectives

Paras 3 and 4 pp. 148–9

3   a   **pulchrum** (singular neuter nominative)

    b   **fortis** (singular masculine genitive)

    c   **ingentia** (plural neuter accusative)

    d   **bonae** (singular feminine dative)

4   a   The young man easily overpowered the savage lion.
        leōnem saevum: singular masculine accusative
    b   The priests offered a sacrifice to the immortal gods.
        dīs immortālibus: plural masculine dative
    c   The friend saw the ship of the honest merchant.
        mercātōris probī: singular masculine genitive
    d   The wise women hid the money.
        fēminae sapientēs: plural feminine nominative
    e   The doctor examined the eyes of the sick soldiers.
        mīlitum aegrōrum: plural masculine genitive
    f   He bought a huge building near the river.
        aedificium ingēns: singular neuter accusative

Further work **SSB p. 14**

bonus, bona, bonum	fortis, forte	ingēns, *gen.* ingentis
attonitus, attonita, attonitum	trīstis, trīste	sapiēns, *gen.* sapientis
stultus, stulta, stultum	dulcis, dulce	furēns, *gen.* furentis

Stage 22 dēfīxiō

Model sentences

Translation pp. 22–3

1 A thief cautiously entered the baths. The thief, having entered the baths, hurried to the sacred spring.

2 The thief, standing near the spring, looked around. The thief, having caught sight of an old man, hid (himself) behind a pillar.

3 The old man, holding a gold amulet (lucky charm), advanced to the spring. The old man raised his hands to heaven and asked for help from the goddess Sulis.

4 The old man, having prayed to the goddess, threw the amulet into the spring and went out.

5 The thief, who had seen the gold amulet, came back to the spring. The thief, having returned to the spring, looked for the amulet in the water.

6 The thief, having obtained the amulet, read in astonishment: 'DEATH TO ALL THIEVES'. The thief threw down the amulet and fled from the baths in terror.

Questions SSB pp. 16–17

Sentences 1

The thief hurried to the sacred spring. He entered the baths. His intention was probably to trawl the water for coins, etc., thrown in by visitors.

Sentences 2

a The thief, standing near the spring, looked around.

b He hid behind a pillar. **senem cōnspicātus** (*having caught sight of an old man*).

Sentences 3

a Holding a gold amulet (lucky charm).

b The old man **raised his hands** to heaven and **asked for help** from the goddess Sulis.

Sentence 4

The old man threw the amulet in the water, after he had prayed to the goddess (*lit.* having prayed to the goddess). The old man may have hoped that his offering would persuade the goddess to answer his prayer.

Sentences 5

a The thief had seen the gold amulet.

b The thief, having returned to the spring, looked for the amulet in the water.

Sentences 6

a **amulētum adeptus** (*having obtained the amulet*).

b The thief was not expecting the amulet to be inscribed with a curse 'Death to all thieves'.

c He left empty-handed / He was terrified by the curse on the amulet.

Vilbia SSB pp. 17–18

Questions lines 1–10

1 Vilbia and Rubria are sisters.

2 Latro is very hardworking, but has very little sense (*lit.* a man of great diligence, but of very little sense).

3 The wine-cups are dirty because Vilbia and Rubria are chatting instead of doing the washing up.

4 *Vilbia … did not obey her father.* She did not get on with the washing up; instead, she showed a brooch to Rubria.

Further work

1 present participle: **lavantēs**.

2 nouns in the genitive case; two of: **tabernae**, **Latrōnis**, **dīligentiae**, **prūdentiae**.

3 imperative: **labōrāte** or **nōlīte (garrīre)**.

4 comparative adjective: **loquāciōrēs**.

Questions lines 11–31

1 The brooch is beautiful and expensive, and Rubria thinks it is silver.

2 Modestus, a Roman soldier, gave it to Vilbia.

3 Rubria thinks that Roman soldiers in general are deceitful and cowardly.

4 Vilbia says that he once killed three thousand of the enemy and that he now guards the commander himself.

5 No; Rubria remarks sarcastically that Modestus is another Hercules (for this legendary hero, see the answer to **Modestus**, question 9, below) and that she has often heard a story of similar (exaggerated) exploits from other soldiers.

6 Modestus visited their pub.

7 Vilbia was attracted by the size of his shoulders and arms.

8 Bulbus is Vilbia's former boyfriend. Rubria warns her sister that it is dangerous to reject him, because he understands magic.

9 Vilbia complains that Bulbus often talked of marriage, but never did anything about it. Modestus, on the other hand, who is very strong and very daring, is able to look after her. She describes Bulbus as a scoundrel (**pestem**), but Modestus as her heart-throb (**suspīrium**).

10 *Naïve*: She believes without question all Modestus tells her about his marvellous exploits, despite the warnings of her more experienced sister.

Shallow: She is swayed entirely by the beauty of the silver brooch and by Modestus' physique.

Unfaithful: She is so carried away by the excitement of the handsome soldier's arrival that she scorns her previous love. However, as Bulbus does not want to settle down, perhaps she is right to look elsewhere.

Foolish: She transfers her affections without a second thought to Modestus, without knowing anything more about him than his highly questionable boasting. This also leads her to reject her previous boyfriend despite his potentially dangerous understanding of magic.

Modestus

Translation p. 25

Modestus and Strythio are walking to Latro's pub. Although Strythio is a friend of Modestus, he is making fun of him.

Modestus: Where are you, Strythio? I order you to stand near me.

Strythio: I'm here. By Hercules! How lucky I am! I am standing near a very courageous man. For you are braver than Mars himself.

Modestus: You speak the truth. Once I killed three thousand of the enemy.

Strythio: All the girls love you, because you are so brave and handsome. That Vilbia, having caught sight of you yesterday, fell in love immediately. She asked a lot about you.

Modestus: What did she say?

Strythio: She asked me eagerly, 'Is he Hercules?' 'No! He's his brother', I answered. Then I handed Vilbia the brooch that another girl had given to you. 'Modestus, a kind and noble man', I said, 'is giving you this brooch free.' Vilbia, having received the brooch, replied to me, 'How handsome Modestus is! How generous! I should like to have a chat with him.'

Modestus: Oh dear! Girls are troublesome, aren't they? It is difficult for me to avoid girls. I'm too handsome.

Strythio: Look! We've arrived at Latro's pub. Perhaps Vilbia is in, who adores you like a god.
(*They enter the pub.*)

Questions SSB p. 18

1 Modestus expects Strythio to be on hand the moment he needs him and to do exactly as he orders him.

2 He says he is lucky to be standing next to a man of the greatest courage, who is braver than Mars himself.

3 He claims that he once killed three thousand of the enemy.

4 Vilbia, having caught sight of him yesterday, immediately fell in love with him and has asked a lot of questions about him.

5 Another girl had given it to him.

6 Having received the brooch, Vilbia responded by exclaiming how handsome and generous Modestus was and how much she would like to talk with him.

7 He is very arrogant and conceited, complaining that it is difficult for him to avoid girls, whom he finds irritating, because he is too handsome.

8   They arrive at Latro's pub.

9   Mars was the god of war and therefore incredibly powerful, strong and brave – an especially flattering comparison for a soldier. Hercules was a legendary Greek hero who completed twelve extraordinarily difficult labours, including slaying a monster and descending to the Underworld to retrieve the three-headed guard-dog Cerberus. He was also, therefore, renowned for amazing strength and courage.

10 **tū enim fortior es quam Mārs ipse** (lines 5–6): comparing Modestus to the god of war is very much to exaggerate his prowess.

    tē omnēs puellae amant (line 8): again, exaggerating and playing on Modestus' high opinion of his own good looks.

    minimē! est frāter eius (lines 12–13): making fun of Modestus' pretensions to being a second Hercules and Vilbia's eagerness to believe him.

    tē tamquam deum adōrat (line 22): making fun of Modestus' inflated opinion of himself and his effect on girls.

About the language 1: perfect active participles p. 26 SSB p. 19

1   The participles are perfect **passive** participles (*having been ...ed*).

2   The participles are perfect **active** participles (*having ...ed*).

Picture question

a   The amulet, (**having been**) **thrown** into the water, was made of gold.

b   The thief, **having returned** to the spring, found the amulet in the water.

regressus is the perfect active participle.

3   a   Modestus, having entered the pub, caught sight of Vilbia.

    b   Vilbia, having spoken many words, was silent at last.

    c   The merchants, having received the money, hurried to their ships.

d   The woman, having prayed to the goddess Sulis, threw the amulet into the spring.

e   The slave-girls, having caught sight of the ring, wanted to look at it.

	Participle	Noun	Number
a	ingressus	Modestus	singular
b	locūta	Vilbia	singular
c	adeptī	mercātōrēs	plural
d	precāta	fēmina	singular
e	cōnspicātae	ancillae	plural

amor omnia vincit

scaena prīma

Translation p. 27 SSB p. 20

Bulbus and his friend are in Latro's pub. They are drinking wine and playing dice. Bulbus owes his friend a lot of money.

Gutta: (*friend of Bulbus*) How unlucky you are! Not only have you lost your girl, but also your money.

Bulbus: **I do not care about the money, but I do not want to lose my Vilbia.**

Gutta: How can you hold on to her? A Roman soldier, a man of outstanding bravery, is after her. Hey! I've thrown a Venus! Innkeeper! I order you to bring more wine.

Bulbus: **The soldier, who has deceived her, is a lying and cowardly man. Vilbia, (having been) deceived by him, now rejects me. I often warned her, 'Don't trust soldiers, especially Roman ones.' Vilbia, however, having caught sight of this Modestus, immediately fell in love with him.**

Gutta: It's not safe for girls to go through the streets of this town. Such (so great) is the cheek of these soldiers. Good heavens! You are even more unlucky. You've thrown a dog again. You owe me another denarius.

Bulbus: **I willingly hand over a denarius, not my girl. I hate that soldier. Modestus, however, cannot keep my girl, because I have asked for help from the goddess. Having prayed to the goddess, I threw a tablet into the sacred spring. A dreadful curse, (having been) written on the tablet, now lies in the goddess' spring.** (*Enter Modestus and Strythio, whom Bulbus does not see.*) **I happily await the death of Modestus.**

Gutta: Good heavens! You are very unlucky. Look! Modestus himself is coming towards us. I must leave as quickly as possible.
(*Exit, running.*)

Questions **SSB p. 21**

1 His name is Modestus. Gutta describes him as a man of the greatest courage, which contrasts with Bulbus' opinion of him in lines 10–11 as a lying and cowardly man. Gutta is not really serious and is probably being sarcastic, given his opinion in lines 15–16 that it is not safe for girls to go through the streets of this town because of the arrogance of the soldiers.

2 a Venerem iactāvī!
      I have thrown a Venus!
      I've thrown a double six.

   b canem iterum iactāvistī.
      You have thrown a dog again.
      You've thrown a double one.

3 **īnfēlīx**   *unlucky*
   īnfēlīcior   *more unlucky*
   īnfēlīcissimus   *very unlucky*

4 Modestus and Strythio have come into the pub, but Bulbus has not seen them. They have overheard Bulbus saying that he is joyfully looking forward to Modestus' death. As Modestus comes towards Bulbus and Gutta, the latter decides to run for it while leaving Bulbus to his fate. Bulbus is indeed **īnfēlīcissimus**.

scaena secunda   SSB p. 21
Questions

1 Modestus orders Strythio to beat this scoundrel and throw him out of the pub.

2

Description	Character
invītus	Strythio
fortiter	Bulbus
ferōciter	Modestus

3 a *The bravest*: Bulbus, who defends himself bravely by pouring wine onto Strythio's head, despite being attacked unawares by the two men. He is knocked out in the fight, but manages to recover his composure sufficiently to overhear Modestus and Vilbia arranging to meet that night.

   b *The most cowardly*: Modestus, who first of all orders Strythio to do his dirty work for him and only then joins in the fight by hitting Bulbus violently as soon as his back is turned.

4 Vilbia continues to be unfaithful in rejecting and insulting Bulbus (**rīdiculus mūs** *a silly mouse*) in favour of the apparently brave Modestus (**tū es leō.** *You are a lion.*). She is foolish in continuing to believe in Modestus' bravery, just because he is a Roman soldier, and in failing to see through his pomposity (**victōribus decōrum est victīs parcere.** *It is right for winners to spare the conquered.*). She is shallow and easily flattered by Modestus' attentions (**cūr mē ex omnibus puellīs ēlēgistī? quam laeta sum!** *Why have you chosen me out of all the girls? How happy I am!*). She is naïve in going along with Modestus' plan to meet secretly by night. Here again she disobeys her father.

   Compare your answer and the points made above with your discussion of her character in **Vilbia** p. 24 (SSB pp. 17–18).

5 a Bulbus had been knocked out by Modestus.

   b He will have especially noted when and where Modestus and Vilbia are intending to meet: **noctū** *by night*; **in locō sēcrētō** *in a secret place* (line 19); **prope fontem deae Sūlis** *near the spring of the goddess Sulis* (line 22).

scaena tertia

Translation lines 1–13 p. 29

In the silence of the night, Bulbus and Gutta enter the baths. They hide (themselves) near the sacred spring. Bulbus shows Gutta a dress and a cloak, which he has brought with him.

Bulbus: Gutta, I want you to put on these clothes. I want you to play the part of Vilbia. We must deceive Modestus, whom I expect in a short time.

Gutta: Ugh! It is not proper for a man to wear a dress. Besides, I have a beard.

Bulbus: That is of very little importance, because we are in darkness. Surely I can persuade you? Look! I'm giving you ten denarii. Now be quiet! Put on the dress and cloak! Stand near the goddess' spring! When Modestus approaches the spring, say the sweetest words to him!

Questions lines 14–end SSB p. 22

1 Gutta is standing near the spring, having reluctantly put on the dress. Modestus approaches the spring, having entered the baths alone.

2 Modestus suggests that Vilbia's voice is hoarse from crying because he arrived late. (Really, of course, it is Gutta's voice.)

3 Modestus approaches 'Vilbia' in order to dry her tears and comes up against a beard.

4 **fortissimus mīlitum** means *the bravest of soldiers*. In lines 27–31, Modestus reacts to being thrown into the spring by shouting 'I'm dying' and 'Spare me!' He is ready instantly to return Vilbia to Bulbus when faced with the threat of being killed. He does not seem to be very brave at all.

5 Vilbia is terrified by the sound of shouting when she enters the baths. (Bulbus has just thrown Modestus into the spring.) Her fear turns to anger when she hears Modestus say that he does not love her.

6 Modestus spoke these words to Vilbia when standing over Bulbus in **scaena secunda** (p. 28, line 15). Bulbus would repeat them in a sarcastic or humorous tone, reminding Vilbia gently of her naïve belief in Modestus' noble feelings when he spoke them to her. Bulbus might even imitate Modestus' original pompous tone. Vilbia would realise that she was foolish to fall so easily for Modestus and that it was Bulbus who was really brave and whom she really loved.

7 Bulbus and Vilbia end up being the winners in rediscovering their love for each other, with Vilbia perhaps learning her lesson after her foolishness nearly drove them apart. Gutta is also a winner as he leaves happily counting his money. Modestus is definitely the loser as he leaves the spring with nothing but wet clothes. Strythio may be a loser if Modestus takes out his humiliation on him.

About the language 2: more about the genitive

Translation p. 31

3 a too much money

   b no danger

   c more work

   d much / a lot of water

Further work SSB p. 22

Latin phrase	Translation
nimium clāmōris	too much noise
plūs cibī	more food
nihil artis	no art/skill
aliquid praemiī	some reward
multum negōtiī	a lot of business

5   a   a man of very little sense / a very foolish man (*or similar*)

     b   a young man of twenty years / a young man, aged twenty *or* twenty years old

     c   a woman of great wisdom / a very wise woman

     d   a story of this kind / this kind of story / a story like this

     e   a girl of very great cleverness / a very clever girl

     f   a man of very good character / a very good man

Further work SSB p. 23

1   mīles summae virtūtis

2   uxor ingeniī optimī

3   fūr ingeniī prāvī

4   ancilla maximae calliditātis

5   cōnsilium huius modī

6   faber minimae prūdentiae

Magic and curses SSB p. 23

1   On the face of it Modestus' downfall seems to be due not to the curse, but to Bulbus' clever trick in catching Modestus off his guard at the sacred spring. On the other hand, Bulbus might argue that his curse had persuaded the goddess to make his plan work perfectly. After all, Vilbia might have come in early and ruined Bulbus' plan.

2   Free choice. Most curse tablets were attached to a tomb or thrown into a well or spring.

Word patterns: more adjectives and adverbs

Paras 3–5 p. 32

3	*adjectives*		*adverbs*	
	suāvis	*sweet*	suāviter	***sweetly***
	neglegēns	***careless***	neglegenter	*carelessly*
	audāx	***bold***	audācter	***boldly***

4	*adjectives*		*adverbs*	
	fortis	*brave*	fortiter	*bravely*
	fidēlis	*faithful*	fidēliter	*faithfully*
	īnsolēns	*rude*	īnsolenter	*rudely*
	sapiēns	*wise*	sapienter	*wisely*

5   a   sensible   **prūdēns**

     b   quickly   **celeriter**

     c   happy   **laetus**

     d   diligently   **dīligenter**

     e   very cruelly   **crūdēlissimē**

Further work SSB p. 23

1   a   The adverbs derived from 1st and 2nd declension adjectives end in **-ē**.

     b   The adverbs derived from 3rd declension adjectives end in **-ter**.

2   *1st/2nd declensions*

adjectives		*adverbs*	
benignus	*kind*	benignē	*kindly*
malus	*bad*	malē	*badly*
pessimus	*very bad*	pessimē	*very badly*

3rd declension

adjectives		*adverbs*	
crūdēlis	*cruel*	crūdēliter	*cruelly*
gravis	*serious*	graviter	*seriously*
ēlegāns	*elegant*	ēleganter	*elegantly*

Practising the language p. 33

1   a   Modestus per viās **oppidī** ambulābat, puellam quaerēns.

         Modestus was walking through the streets of the town, looking for a girl.

     b   Gutta, vir benignus, auxilium **amīcō** saepe dabat.

         Gutta, a kind man, often helped (lit. gave help to) his friend.

     c   Rubria, quae in tabernā labōrābat, **iuvenī** vīnum obtulit.

         Rubria, who was working in the pub, offered wine to the young man.

     d   prope vīllam **haruspicis**, turba ingēns conveniēbat.

         Near the soothsayer's house, a huge crowd was gathering.

     e   tabernārius **ancillīs** multās rēs pretiōsās ostendit.

         The shopkeeper showed many precious things to the slave-girls.

f clāmōrēs **fabrōrum** architectum
vexāvērunt.
The shouts of the workmen annoyed the
architect.

g centuriō gladiōs hastāsque **mīlitum**
īnspicere coepit.
The centurion began to inspect the soldiers'
swords and spears.

h caupō vīnum pessimum **hospitibus**
offerēbat.
The innkeeper used to offer very bad wine to
his guests.

2 **a** subitō ancilla **perterrita** in ātrium irrūpit.
Suddenly the terrified slave-girl burst into the
atrium.

b rēx, postquam hoc audīvit, fabrōs **fessōs**
dīmīsit.
After the king heard this, he sent away the
tired workmen.

c senātor quī aderat iuvenēs **callidōs**
laudāvit.
The senator who was present praised the
clever young men.

d omnēs cīvēs nāvem **sacram** spectābant.
All the citizens were looking at the sacred
ship.

e ubi in magnō perīculō eram, amīcus
fidēlis mē servāvit.
When I was in great danger, a faithful friend
saved me.

f 'in illā īnsulā', inquit senex, 'habitant
multī virī **ferōcēs**.'
'On that island', said the old man, 'live many
ferocious men.'

g fēmina **fortis**, quae in vīllā manēbat,
fūrem superāvit.
The brave woman, who was staying in the
house, overcame the thief.

h cīvēs in viīs oppidī **multōs** mīlitēs vidēre
solēbant.
The citizens were accustomed to see many
soldiers in the streets of the town.

Vocabulary checklist 22 SSB p. 24

1 Cupid was the Roman god of love, the young
son of Venus. *Amoretti* are literally *little loves*
(from **amor**).

2 If someone is *eligible*, he or she is suitable
to be chosen, although promotion is not
guaranteed (from **ēligō**).

3 She welcomes you with an outpouring of
emotion (from **fundō**).

4 At the beginning (from **incipiō**).

5 Prone to tears / miserable (from **lacrima**).

6 Bare. A *minimalist* house has very little
furniture or decoration (from **minimus**).

7 An animal who is awake by night, e.g. an owl
(from **nox**).

8 You would probably not enjoy listening
to him as his speech would be full of
(unnecessary) words. If his speech were
reported *verbatim*, it would be reported
word for word (from **verbum**).

9 There is no way the accident could be
avoided (from **vītō**).

10 precātus   *having prayed*
     adeptus   *having received*
     dēceptus   *having been deceived*
     ingressus *having entered*
dēceptus is the odd one out, because it is a
perfect *passive* participle (from **dēcipiō**). The
other three are perfect *active* participles.

Language test SSB p. 25

1 Modestus, having entered the pub, saw
Vilbia. Having caught sight of Modestus, she
at once fell in love with him.
    'Wine, girl!' said Modestus.
    Modestus, having said these words, sat
down. Vilbia, delighted by Modestus, poured
out the wine. Modestus, having got the wine,
said,
    'My darling, how lovely you are! I would
like to get to know you.'

Vilbia, having returned to the kitchen, said,

'O goddess Venus! Having often prayed to you, I give you the greatest thanks / thank you very much because you have sent this wonderful man for me.'

Perfect active participles
ingressus, cōnspicāta, locūtus, adeptus, regressa, precāta.

Perfect passive participle
dēlectāta.

2   a   Memor often used to drink **too much wine**.

b   It is difficult for the goddess to cure **a man eighty years old** (*lit.* **of eighty years**).

c   The friends entered the baths **quietly**.

d   Cephalus announced **some news** to Memor.

e   Latro, **a very stupid man** (*lit.* **a man of very little intelligence**) was always blaming his daughters.

f   Vilbia had never seen **a more handsome man** than Modestus.

Revision

Nouns: genitive and dative cases SSB p. 25

	singular	*plural*
1	puellae	puellīs
2	cīvis	cīvium
3	mercātōrī	mercātōribus
4	puerī	puerōrum
5	servō	servīs

Imperatives SSB p. 26

	translation	*plural*
1	*Be quiet!*	tacēte!
2	*Stand near the goddess' spring!*	stāte prope fontem deae!
3	*Come to me!*	venīte ad mē!
4	*Do not kill me!*	nōlīte mē interficere!
5	*Do not cry!*	nōlīte lacrimāre!

Comparatives and superlatives

Paras 1 and 2 **SSB pp. 26–7**

1

Adjective	Comparative	Superlative
gravis *heavy*	**gravior** *heavier*	**gravissimus** *very heavy*
perfidus *treacherous*	perfidior *more treacherous*	**perfidissimus** *very treacherous*
difficilis *difficult*	**difficilior** *more difficult*	**difficillimus** *very difficult*
potēns *powerful*	potentior *more powerful*	**potentissimus** *very powerful*
celer *quick*	celerior *quicker*	**celerrimus** *very quick*

2   a   bad   **malus**

b   best   **optimus**

c   big   **magnus**

d   more   **plūs**

e   very small   **minimus**

f   many   **multī**

Paras 3 and 4 **p. 151**

3   a   'No one is braver than Modestus', said Vilbia.

b   The procession was very long (and) also very beautiful.

c   You are worse than a thief!

d   Salvius' villa was smaller than Cogidubnus' palace.

e   It was very easy for us to capture the city.

f   I have never visited a better pub/shop than yours.

g   Memor wanted to rise to greater public positions/honours.

h   In the middle of the town were working very many craftsmen who were building a very large temple.

4   a   Bregans was the most stupid of all the slaves that Salvius had.

b   All my soldiers are brave; you, however, are the bravest.

c   Finally we visited Athens, the most beautiful of all cities.

Stage 23 haruspex

in thermīs I SSB pp. 29–30

Questions

1 a The temple was near the baths; it had been built by the craftsmen of Cogidubnus.

   b The altar was in front of the temple and was huge.

2 The ceremony was taking place at the altar (in front of the temple).

3 a Quintus was standing near the king's chair.

   b A band of soldiers was guarding them.

   c Memor was wearing a fine toga.

4 He was trembling with nervousness in case the omens were unfavourable and his plot to kill the king was discovered.

5 a templum … aedificātum.

   b Memor … gerēns; sacerdōtēs … dūcentēs.

   c *Two of*: Cogidubnī; rēgis; mīlitum.

6 The priest thought that the lead-coloured liver indicated the death of a famous man. **nōnne** (*surely*).

7 Memor did not agree with the priest. He answered 'No' and went on to say that the goddess had sent them very good omens.

8 He interpreted the omens as excellent; they indicated a remarkable cure for Cogidubnus because the goddess (Sulis Minerva) favoured him.

9 Then Memor led the king and his chieftains into the changing-room.

10 a nōbīs; tibi.

   b quī perterritus pallēscēbat.
      quae precēs aegrōtōrum audīre solet.

   c locūtus.

Further work

1 āram **omnēs** aspiciēbant.
   Everyone was looking towards the altar.

2 agnam **sacerdōs** sacrificāvit.
   The priest sacrificed the lamb.

3 iecur agnae **haruspex** īnspexit.
   The soothsayer inspected the liver of the lamb.

4 nōnne mortem **hoc** significat?
   Surely this indicates a death?

Roman religion SSB p. 30

1 The sacrifice is important because three expensive animals are to be sacrificed; a tall impressive figure is making the sacrifice (we are told that it is the emperor in his role of Chief Priest); he is accompanied by a solemn procession (which in reality was probably longer than can be shown on a carving like this).

2 The man about to kill the animals (**popa**) is second on the left, holding an axe.

3 The people are wearing garlands on their heads and the bull is decorated with a patterned ribbon.

4 The incense smoke would rise to the gods in heaven and both honour and please them because it was expensive and sweet-smelling.

in thermīs II SSB pp. 30–1

1

Line	Word or phrase	Reason
3	attonitus	Quintus (when he saw the biggest bath) was astonished because he thought the baths were bigger than those at Pompeii.
6	cum magnā difficultāte	The slaves experienced great difficulty in lowering Cogidubnus into the bath. He was old and ill and probably found it difficult to move.
7	maximus clāmor	The noise was loud because the king was giving instructions to his chieftains, the chieftains were cursing their freedmen and the freedmen were cursing the slaves.
12	anxius	Cephalus was anxious because he was about to offer Cogidubnus the poisoned cup.

2   **A** temple   **B** altar
      C spring   **D** the Great Bath

3

Line	Character	Actions
16	Cephalus	offered the cup to the king.
16–17	Cogidubnus	raised the cup to his lips.
18	Quintus	caught sight of the cup; he grasped the king's hand as he was raising the cup to his lips.
19–21	Quintus	shouted, 'Don't drink! This is a poisoned cup. I have seen a cup of this sort in the city of Alexandria.'
22	Quintus	began to inspect the cup.
22–3	Cephalus	tried to snatch the cup from Quintus' hands.
24–5	Dumnorix	seized the cup and offered it to Cephalus.

4   **a** Dumnorix meant that if the cup merely contained water, there was no need for Cephalus to fear drinking from it. His tone might be challenging or sarcastic.

    b Cephalus would have aroused suspicion by refusing to drink from the cup and by falling down at the knees of the king.

    c The king is described as **immōtus**, probably because he was so stunned at the turn of events and could not believe what was happening.

    d The chieftains seized the freedman and forced him to drink from the cup.

    e **mortuus** (*dead*).

Further work

These baths are smaller/better/worse than the Pompeian baths.

These baths are the smallest/best/worst *or* very small / very good / very bad.

About the language 1: more about participles p. 41 SSB p. 32

1–3 Present, perfect passive, perfect active.

4 a The king, sitting in the middle of the crowd, greeted the chieftains.

b The freedman, having returned to the bedroom, tried to wake up Memor.

c Vilbia showed Rubria the brooch given by Modestus.

d The priests, having prayed to the goddess, sacrificed the lamb.

e The temple, built by the Romans, was near the sacred spring.

f The sisters, working in the pub, caught sight of the soldier.

g The thief looked for things thrown into the spring.

h Some slave-girls, beaten by their mistress, obtained poison.

	Noun	Participle	Description
a	rēx	sedēns	present
b	lībertus	regressus	perfect active
c	fībulam	datam	perfect passive
d	sacerdōtēs	precātī	perfect active
e	templum	aedificātum	perfect passive
f	sorōrēs	labōrantēs	present
g	rēs	iniectās	perfect passive
h	ancillae	verberātae	perfect passive

5

	Singular/plural
a	singular
b	singular
c	singular
d	plural
e	singular
f	plural
g	plural
h	plural

Roman religion continued SSB pp. 32–3

1

Roman deity	Greek deity	Characteristics, spheres of influence
Jupiter	Zeus	the king of the gods, the sky and weather
Juno	Hera	wife of Jupiter, fertility, marriage, women
Minerva	Athene	wisdom, crafts, war, patron of Athens
Ceres	Demeter	fertility of the earth, crops
Apollo	Phoebus, (Apollon)	the sun, archery, music and the arts
Mars	Ares	war
Mercury	Hermes	messenger of the gods, commerce

2 a Mercury/Hermes

b Jupiter/Zeus

c Apollo/Phoebus (Apollon)

3 a Skills in combat and defence are called *martial* arts.

b Grain crops are sometimes called *cereals*.

c Someone with a cheerful disposition, like Jove, is said to be *jovial*.

epistula Cephalī SSB p. 34

1

Line	Statement	T/F	Reason
3	Memor īnsānit.	F	Memor was worried and asked Cephalus' advice, but he was not mad.
9	"Imperātor mortem Cogidubnī cupit", inquit (Memor).	T	Memor is repeating what Salvius told him. He has accepted it as true.
10	"iubeō tē venēnum parāre."	F	The poison was Cephalus' idea.
12–13	Memorī respondī, "longē errās. Cogidubnus est vir ingeniī optimī."	F	Cephalus said nothing about Cogidubnus' character, but immediately suggested a way of killing him.
19–20	Memor custōdem arcessīvit, quī mē verberāvit.	F	This had not been necessary. Cephalus had thought out the plan and had reluctantly agreed to carry it out.
24	Memor coēgit mē hanc rem efficere.	F	Cephalus protested, but was not forced by Memor to murder Cogidubnus.

2 Cephalus obviously wanted to throw the blame for the murder plan on Memor, as you will see from your answers to question 1. Did he mean the letter to be delivered only if he (Cephalus) were incriminated in the murder or attempted murder, or did he mean it to be an advance warning to Cogidubnus before he entered the baths? In this case the slave must have delivered it late because the murder attempt had been made and Cephalus was already dead. Perhaps Cephalus intended that, even if he died, he could take revenge on Memor for the way he had been treated in the past.

About the language 2: the plural of neuter nouns p. 43 SSB p. 34

1–2 The accusative of a neuter noun is the same as its nominative. All neuter plurals end in –**a**.

3
  a The building was very magnificent.
  b When he heard these words, Memor fell silent.
  c The doctor inspected the soldier's wound.
  d Cephalus suddenly had an idea.
  e These bedrooms are very dirty.
  f The slaves brought drinking cups to the chieftains.

Further work

1 **a** The temples are splendid.
     nominative plural
  b The girl is very happy.
     nominative singular
2 **a** I often visited the temples in Britain.
     accusative plural
  b The girl often visited her mother.
     nominative singular

Britannia perdomita

Questions p. 45

		Marks
1	Salvius.	1
2	The king is wearing a splendid toga and precious decorations.	1
	He is at the head of a large number of armed men.	1
3	Salvius thinks that Cogidubnus (suspects them and) is seeking revenge.	1
4	Memor is a Roman, like himself, while Cogidubnus is a barbarian.	1
5	Cogidubnus accuses Memor of plotting against him. Memor ordered Cephalus to obtain poison and kill him.	3
6	Cephalus is dead.	1

7   Cogidubnus' proof is a letter written
    by Cephalus (in which he revealed
    everything). A slave (sent by Cephalus)
    brought it to him.   2

8   The slave suffered many tortures
    but has stuck to his story.   1

9   'Why did you bring armed men here?'   1

10 Salvius has kept silent because he has
    been thinking what to do next / He
    wants to hear exactly what Cogidubnus
    knows about the plan to murder him.   1

11 Cogidubnus has told him that he has
    been sacked from managing the baths.   1

12 Salvius says that Cogidubnus obtained
    the highest honours from the Romans.
    But he had never been content. Now
    he was openly showing his treachery.   3

13 Salvius says that he has been ordered
    to take over Cogidubnus' kingdom.   1
    The order came from the Emperor
    Domitian.   1

14 Cogidubnus is throwing his decorations
    to the ground.   1
    He is showing his contempt for them
    / He no longer wants to be associated
    with the Romans (or similar).   1

15 *Memor*
    Beginning:
    He must feel safe because Cephalus has been
    blamed for the attempted murder / because
    Cephalus is dead.
    End:
    He has been found out / Even if Salvius
    supports him, he is a marked man.
    Salvius
    Beginning:
    He is described as anxious because the plot
    has failed.
    End:
    He goes on the attack against Cogidubnus /
    He uses Cogidubnus' outburst to put him in
    the wrong / He sees his chance to take over
    the kingdom of the Regnenses.

Cogidubnus
Beginning:
He is very angry because he has discovered
Memor's plot against him / (As a client king
and a Roman citizen) he comes to confront
Memor.
End:
Salvius attacks him instead of supporting
him / He is very bitter because the Romans
have betrayed him / The Romans are about
to take over his kingdom.
You may have thought of other good answers. 3

TOTAL 25

Further work SSB p. 35

1   a   What you say is ridiculous.
    b   Cephalus was a very sensible man.
    c   I have already removed Memor from
        being in charge of the baths.
    d   No men are more treacherous than the
        Romans.

2   a   *One of*: parāvistī, iussistī, dedistī, dūxistī,
        dēmōvistī, fēcistī, fuistī.
    b   *One of*: epistulam scrīptam, servus
        missus, ōrnāmenta data.
    c   *One of*: servus ingressus, Cogidubnus
        suspicātus, servus passus, tū adeptus,
        Imperātor Domitiānus passus.
    d   *One of*: ōrnāmenta, mandāta, tormenta.

3   a   Cogidubnus had for years supported
        the Romans and had adopted their way
        of life, thus helping with their policy of
        romanisation. He did not deserve to be
        suddenly abandoned and mistreated.
    b   He was willing to aid and support a
        foreign invader and ready to accept
        rewards and honours even though it was
        disloyal to his own people. He was happy
        to adopt Roman customs and religion
        and abandon the British way of life.

You may have thought of other good
answers. You could also feel sorry for
Cogidubnus and at the same time think that
he should have known how ruthless the
Romans could be.

Word patterns: verbs and nouns p. 46 SSB p. 36

2 *Infinitive*

emere	*to buy*
legere	**to read**
spectāre	**to watch**

Perfect passive participle

ēmptus
lēctus
spectātus

Noun

ēmptor	**buyer**
lēctor	*reader*
spectātor	*spectator/onlooker*

3 defender, seller, traitor, lover.

4

English noun	Perfect passive participle	Infinitive
demonstrator	dēmōnstrātus	dēmōnstrāre
curator	cūrātus	cūrāre
navigator	nāvigātus	nāvigāre
narrator	nārrātus	nārrāre
tractor	tractus	trahere
doctor	doctus	docēre

Picture caption: **caveat ēmptor** means *Let the buyer beware.*

5 The ending **-or** here means a person or thing carrying out a particular action or function.

Further work

Latin noun	Perfect passive participle	Infinitive
dēfēnsor	dēfēnsus	dēfendere
vēnditor	vēnditus	vēndere
prōditor	prōditus	prōdere
amātor	amātus	amāre

Picture question: F.D. on a coin means *Defender of the Faith.* It is one of the titles of the British king or queen.

Practising the language p. 47 SSB p. 37

1 a nōs ancillae fessae sumus; semper in vīllā **labōrāmus**.
We slave-girls are tired; we are always working in the house.

b 'quid faciunt illī servī?' 'pōcula ad mīlitēs **ferunt**.'
'What are those slaves doing?' 'They are carrying/bringing wine-cups to the soldiers.'

c fīlius meus vōbīs grātiās agere vult, quod mē **servāvistis**.
My son wants to thank you, because you saved me.

d quamquam prope āram **stābāmus**, sacrificium vidēre nōn poterāmus.
Although we were standing near the altar, we could not see the sacrifice.

e ubi prīncipēs fontī **appropinquābant**, Cephalus prōcessit, pōculum tenēns.
When the chieftains were approaching the spring, Cephalus advanced, holding the wine-cup.

f in maximō perīculō estis, quod fīlium rēgis **interfēcistis**.
You are in very great danger because you have killed the king's son.

g nōs, quī fontem sacrum numquam **vīderāmus**, ad thermās cum rēge īre cupiēbāmus.
We, who had never seen the sacred spring, wanted to go to the baths with the king.

h dominī nostrī sunt benignī; nōbīs semper satis cibī **praebent**.
Our masters are kind; they always provide enough food for us.

2 *Perfect active participles*

adeptus	*having obtained*
locūtus	*having spoken*
ingressus	*having entered*

Perfect passive participles

missus	*having been sent*
excitātus	*having been woken*
superātus	*having been overcome*

a Cogidubnus, haec verba **locūtus**, ab aulā discessit.

Cogidubnus, having said these words, left the palace.

b nūntius, ab amīcīs meīs **missus**, epistulam mihi trādidit.

The messenger, (having been) sent by my friends, handed over the letter to me.

c fūr, vīllam **ingressus**, cautē circumspectāvit.

The thief, having entered the house, looked round cautiously.

d Bulbus, ā Modestō **superātus**, sub mēnsā iacēbat.

Bulbus, (having been) overcome by Modestus, was lying under the table.

e haruspex, ā Cephalō **excitātus**, ē lectō surrēxit.

The soothsayer, (having been) woken by Cephalus, got up out of bed.

f mīles, amulētum **adeptus**, in fontem iniēcit.

The soldier, having obtained the amulet, threw it into the spring.

Vocabulary p. 169

5 adiuvāre *to help*; comprehēnsus *having been arrested/seized*; nocēre *to hurt/harm*; pāreō *I obey*; patefēcī *I (have) revealed*; prōditus *having been betrayed*; suscēpī *I have undertaken, I undertook*; victus *having been conquered.*

Vocabulary checklist 23 SSB p. 37

1 The opponent would be giving way to you (from **cēdō**).

2 c. A *curator* literally means a person who cares for or is in charge of something. It has come to be associated with museum and art collections (from **cūra**).

3 They receive degrees given to honour their position and achievements, without necessarily having attended a course of study at the university.

4 c. *Elocution*, like *eloquent*, comes from **locūtus**.

5 He had been given an instruction or order.

6 A way of life/living, as in 'Playing computer games became a *modus vivendi*.'

7 The purpose of *ornaments* is to decorate.

8 No, because it would mean his condition had returned to its earlier state (from **regressus**).

9 Knowledge. *Science* comes from **scio**; the noun is **scientia**.

10 Snakes, because their bite can be poisonous.

11 **pārēre** *to obey*; **parāre** *to prepare*.

12 **umquam** *ever*; **enim** *for*; **tālis** *such*; **nimium** *too much.*

Language test SSB p. 38

1

Nominative singular	Accusative singular	Accusative plural	Gender
toga	**togam**	togās	feminine
rēx	rēgem	**rēgēs**	masculine
dōnum	**dōnum**	dōna	neuter
īnsula	īnsulam	**īnsulās**	feminine
custōs	**custōdem**	custōdēs	masculine
flūmen	**flūmen**	flūmina	neuter
mandātum	mandātum	**mandāta**	neuter
lībertus	**lībertum**	lībertōs	masculine

2 **a** The chieftains, having entered with the king, were sitting in front of the temple.

b The priests, leading the victim, advanced to the altar.

c Memor, standing near the altar, inspected the omens.

d The king and the chieftains, having followed Memor, entered the baths.

e The king, having left the bath, put on his clothes.

f Cephalus was standing near the spring, holding a wine-cup.

g The spectators, having caught sight of this, stood motionless.

h The chieftains seized the resisting freedman / the freedman who was resisting.

i Cephalus, forced by the chieftains, drank the poison.

j The freedman, trembling violently, fell down dead.

	Noun	Participle	s./pl.
a	prīncipēs	ingressī	plural
b	sacerdōtēs	dūcentēs	plural
c	Memor	stāns	singular
d	rēx, prīncipēs	secūtī	plural
e	rēx	ēgressus	singular
f	Cephalus	tenēns	singular
g	spectātōrēs	cōnspicātī	plural
h	lībertum	resistentem	singular
i	Cephalus	coāctus	singular
j	lībertus	tremēns	singular

Revision SSB p. 39

Verbs

Verb	Translation	Tense
gessī	I wore	perfect
ōrnat	s/he decorates	present
scīverant	they had known	pluperfect
pārēbās	you were obeying (s.)	imperfect
cēdunt	they give in	present
iēcistī	you threw (s.)	perfect
gerimus	we are wearing	present
ōrnābātis	you were decorating (pl.)	imperfect
cessērunt	they gave in	perfect
sciēbam	I used to know	imperfect

Pronouns

Further work

1. nōbīs
2. vōs
3. sibi
4. tū, mē
5. nōs, tēcum
6. nōs, sēcum

Stage 24 fuga

In Stage 22, Modestus was described as a brave Roman soldier with a fit body – a real Hercules! He looks quite different in this drawing. There has been no physical description of Strythio up to this point. Here he is depicted as a skinny individual, in contrast to his fat friend. Does this pair of fat and thin comic characters remind you or older members of your family of similar comic partnerships in show business, like Laurel and Hardy, or Little and Large?

in itinere

Questions SSB p. 41

1 **equitābant** (*they were riding*).

2 The river was deep and the bridge was rickety. The horse was unwilling/frightened to cross the bridge.

3 Modestus ordered Strythio to cross first. The solution was not successful because the horse was still unwilling to cross.

4 The horse went across the bridge once Modestus had dismounted.

Translation of lines 9–end   p. 56

'Horse! Come back!' said Modestus. 'You have abandoned me.'

However, the horse stood motionless on the other bank. Modestus began to cross very cautiously. When he had come to the middle of the bridge, down fell the bridge, down fell Modestus. From the middle of the waves he shouted,

'Blockheads, you weakened the bridge.'

SSB p. 41

Note that **cum** means *when*; previously you have met it meaning *with*.

Both phrases mean *from the middle of the waves*.

5 The last sentence is addressed to Strythio and the horse.

Roman bridges SSB pp. 41–2

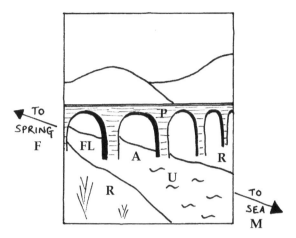

Distinguish between **unda** *wave*; **aqua** *water*; **flūmen** *river*.

Quīntus cōnsilium capit

Questions   p. 59

		Marks
1	Salvius ordered the soldiers to arrest Cogidubnus and the chieftains of the Regnenses and keep them in prison.	2
2	He trusted Quintus. **noctū**.	2
3	Dumnorix wanted Quintus to help him and Cogidubnus.	1
4	He thought most Romans were treacherous / He trusted few Romans.	1
5	Salvius had recently tried to kill Cogidubnus.	1
6	Dumnorix started by flattering Quintus by remarking on his courage and intelligence / He reminded Quintus of his friendship with the king / of the imprisonment of the king / He reminded Quintus that he saved the king previously / He could surely save him again. *Three marks for any three points.*	3
7	Quintus was very fond of the king, but the task was very difficult.	2
8	Quintus suggested they ought to refer the matter secretly to (the governor Gnaeus Julius) Agricola.	1

9 Agricola was in the most distant parts of Britain, fighting a war. 2

10 He held supreme power in Britain. 1

11 The slave provided food for five days. 1

12 *In favour of Quintus*: He was prepared to help Cogidubnus despite the danger / He did not despair in the face of difficulty / He came up with a clever plan / He made intelligent preparations for the journey. *Against Quintus*: He was unwise to try to help Cogidubnus when Salvius was so powerful / He was naive to trust Dumnorix and Cogidubnus / His plan was reckless / What guarantee was there that he would find Agricola / that Agricola would take his side? *Three marks for any three points, for or against Quintus.* 3

TOTAL 20

Further work SSB p. 42

1 Rēgnēnsium; mīlitum.

2 *Two of*: Memoris; Quīntī; Salviī; virtūtis; prūdentiae.

3 *Two of*: mīlitēs … missī; Cogidubnus … comprehēnsus; eum … inclūsum.

4 *Two of*: adiuvā; nōlī (dēserere/relinquere/dēspērāre).

Further questions SSB p. 42

1 Kill him *or* keep him in prison.

2 Dumnorix is loyal to Cogidubnus; he pleads with Quintus to help save Cogidubnus by petitioning Agricola. Dumnorix is brave and impetuous: he has taken the risk of escaping from Salvius' soldiers. As a chieftain of Cogidubnus' tribe of Regnenses, he steered the boat which beat Belimicus and the Cantici (Stage 15); he seized the poisoned wine-cup and made Cephalus drink from it (Stage 23); his taunts roused Belimicus to provoke the bear, but he tried to save Cogidubnus by hurling himself bravely at the bear (Stage 16). He has always acted in Cogidubnus' interests.

3 Quintus saved Cogidubnus from the bear (Stage 16) and prevented him from drinking from the poisoned wine-cup (Stage 23).

4 **illī, ē vīllā ēlāpsī** (*Having escaped from the villa, they*).

About the language 1: *cum* and the pluperfect subjunctive

Para. 3 p. 60

a When the king had gone out, Salvius called the soldiers to him (himself).

b When the gladiators had killed the lion, the spectators applauded.

c When the master had given these orders, the craftsmen returned to the palace.

d The sisters, when they had entered the kitchen, began to wash the dirty wine-cups. *Or*, When the sisters had entered the kitchen, they began to wash the dirty wine-cups.

Further work SSB p. 43

1

Pluperfect singular	*Pluperfect subjunctive singular*	*plural*
ōrnāverat	ōrnā**visset**	ōrnāvissent
monuerat	**monu**isset	monu**issent**
ēlēgerat	ēlē**gisset**	**ēlēgissent**
scīverat	**scīvisset**	**scīvissent**

2 cum Cogidubnus … exiisset. *When Cogidubnus had gone out.* cum Dumnorix … dīxisset. *When Dumnorix had said.* cum … audīvisset. *When he had heard.*

Salvius cōnsilium cognōscit SSB pp. 43–5

1

Line	Action	By whom	Reason
1–2	contenderent	Quintus and Dumnorix	They wanted to reach Agricola quickly and escape from Salvius.
2–3	Dumnorigem … quaerēbant	soldiers	They were searching for Dumnorix under Salvius' orders.
4	vehementer saeviēbat	Salvius	He had found out about Dumnorix's escape.
6	Belimicum … arcessīvit	Salvius	He could not find Quintus anywhere.

2 Salvius said,

'Belimicus, that Dumnorix has escaped from my hands; Quintus Caecilius is also missing. I trust neither Dumnorix nor Quintus. Go now; take soldiers with you; search for them in all parts of the town. Search for their slaves too. It is easy for us to torture slaves and find out the truth in this way.'

Having gone out with many soldiers, Belimicus began to search carefully throughout the town. Meanwhile Salvius was anxiously awaiting his return. When Salvius was thinking over the problem (with himself), Belimicus suddenly returned triumphant. He dragged Quintus' slave into the middle of the hall.

Salvius, having turned to the quivering slave, said,

'Where is Quintus Caecilius? Where has Dumnorix fled to?'

The slave, who, having suffered many tortures, was hardly able to say anything, said,

'I do not know.'

He said again,

'I know nothing.'

When he had heard this, Belimicus drew his sword and held it to the slave's throat. He said,

'It would be better for you to speak the truth to Salvius.'

The slave, who was now despairing for his life, said in a whisper,

'I prepared enough food for five days. I did nothing else. My master departed with Dumnorix into the furthest parts of Britain.'

Salvius said,

'By Hercules! They have gone to Agricola. Quintus, urged on by Dumnorix, is trying to obstruct me; however, he is a man of great stupidity / a very stupid man; he cannot resist me because I have greater authority than he.'

3

	T/F	Reason (if false)
a	F	Salvius gave Belimicus orders, not a reward.
b	T	
c	T	
d	F	Salvius ordered one of his slaves, not his secretary, to take the letter.
e	F	Belimicus followed Quintus and Dumnorix for three days.
f	T	
g	F	Dumnorix died fighting the horsemen. He was not trampled by the horses.
h	F	Quintus escaped with great difficulty.

Travel and communication

SSB pp. 45–6

1 a 120–40 miles. This assumes that Quintus and Dumnorix would have been able to travel between 30 and 35 miles a day. They had taken five days' food with them, which would have been enough if they had been able to manage 35 miles a day.

However, they would have had to stop to sleep and allow the horses to rest and feed; to achieve a good speed they may have had to find fresh horses along the route.

b At least 10 days and probably more. Modestus and Strythio had only one horse to carry them and their packs, so they would have taken at least double the time of a single rider on a fast horse. They probably stopped at wayside pubs for long breaks, which were essential for the horse, if not for them.

2 Large stones (for footing), small stones, rubble, hardcore, material for facing (flints, slag, flat stones), kerbstones.

About the language 2: *cum* and the imperfect subjunctive

Paras 3 and 4   p. 63

3 **a** When the guests were eating the meal, a thief entered the bedroom.

b When the chieftain was considering the matter, the messengers suddenly returned.

c When the young men were hunting the wild beasts, they caught sight of a wounded soldier.

d When the girl was writing a letter, she heard a strange noise.

4 The imperfect subjunctive is a combination of the infinitive and the ending showing the person, here –t and –nt.

Further work SSB p. 46

1 cōnsūmerent; cōgitāret; agitārent; scrīberet.

2 cum … contenderent. *When they were hurrying.*
cum … cōgitāret. *When he was considering.*
cum … īnspicerent. *When they were inspecting.*

3

Present tense	Infinitive	Imperfect subjunctive
adiuvō	adiuvāre	adiuvāret
iubeō	**iubēre**	**iubēret**
scrībō	**scrībere**	**scrīberet**
scio	**scīre**	**scīret**
capiō	**capere**	**caperet**
eō	**īre**	**īret**
possum	**posse**	**posset**
nōlō	**nōlle**	**nōllet**

Travel and communication

continued   SSB p. 47

Picture question

The lighthouse is reminiscent of the Pharos of Alexandria. The purpose of the flags was to show the direction and strength of the wind.

Questions

1 Five types of travellers, e.g. Roman troops; government officials; farm workers; merchants; travellers on private business. There are other possibilities.
Methods of travel: walking; carriages; carts; mules/ponies/horses.

2 Quintus would have to find out from friends or merchants details of distances and stopping places by both land and sea. He might also find a map or handbook to consult. He would try to get in touch with friends who lived near his route so that he did not have to stay at an inn. He would have to arrange transport for himself, his slaves and baggage. He would need suitable travelling clothes and a travelling chest to keep his money and valuables safe.

For the sea voyage he would additionally have to take food and wine for himself and his slaves, and a portable shelter for himself, unless there was a cabin available.

3 *Open question.* If you are in a group, you could take it in turns to read and discuss your accounts of the voyage.

Word patterns: opposites p. 64

SSB p. 47

1
nēmō	*no one*
nusquam	*nowhere*
negōtium	*business*
numquam	*never*

2
impatiēns	*impatient*
inūtilis	*useless*
dissentīre	*to disagree*
difficilis	*difficult*

3
a fēlīx; īnfēlīx
b īnsānus
c amīcus; inimīcus
d similis; dissimilis

4

Latin word	Meaning	Latin opposite
immōtus	motionless	mōtus
incertus	uncertain	certus
dissuādeō	I dissuade	suādeō
incrēdibilis	unbelievable	crēdibilis
nocēns	guilty	innocēns
ignōtus	unknown	nōtus

Practising the language p. 65

1
a medicus puellae **aegrae** pōculum dedit.
The doctor gave a wine-cup to the sick girl.

b hospitēs coquum **callidum** laudāvērunt.
The guests praised the clever cook.

c faber mercātōrī **īrātō** dēnāriōs reddidit.
The craftsman returned the money to the angry merchant.

d ancillae dominō **crūdēlī** pārēre nōlēbant.
The slave-girls were unwilling to obey their cruel master.

e centuriō mīlitēs **ignāvōs** vituperābat.
The centurion was cursing the cowardly soldiers.

f puer stultus nautīs **mendācibus** crēdidit.
The stupid boy trusted the deceitful sailors.

g stolās **novās** emēbat fēmina.
The woman was buying new dresses.

h **omnibus** amīcīs pecūniam obtulī.
I offered money to all the friends.

2
a Quīntus mox ad aulam advēnit. ancilla **eum** in ātrium dūxit.
Quintus soon reached the palace. A slave-girl led him into the atrium.

b Salvius in lectō recumbēbat. puer **eī** plūs cibī obtulit.
Salvius was reclining on a couch. A boy offered more food to him.

c Rūfilla laetissima erat; marītus **eius** tamen nōn erat contentus.
Rufilla was very happy; however, her husband was not content.

d Britannī ferōciter pugnāvērunt, sed Rōmānī tandem **eōs** vīcērunt.
The Britons fought fiercely, but finally the Romans conquered them.

e barbarī impetum in nōs fēcērunt. **eīs** autem restitimus.
The barbarians made an attack on us. However, we resisted them.

f multae fēminae prō templō conveniēbant. līberī **eārum** quoque aderant.
Many women were meeting in front of the temple. Their children were also present.

g prope templum est fōns sacer; **eum** saepe vīsitāvī.
Near the temple is a sacred fountain; I have often visited it.

h in oppidō Aquīs Sūlis erant thermae maximae; architectus Rōmānus **eās** exstrūxit.
There were very big baths in the town of Bath; a Roman builder built them.

Vocabulary checklist 24 SSB p. 48

1 Nelson behaved boldly / with daring (from **audāx**).

2 *Incarceration* means imprisonment (from **carcer**).

3 **comprehendere** means *to seize, catch hold of* someone or something. The verb is also used for seizing or grasping the meaning of something, and therefore means *to understand*. The English derivative is **comprehend** (noun **comprehension**).

4 *When* the king had cursed the Romans, he left *with* his chieftains.

5 **eques** *horseman;* **equus** *horse;* **equitāre** *to ride.*

6 *Posthumously* means after death, originally after burial in the ground (**humī**).

7 Utmost, very great.

8 A *pontoon* is a floating bridge, laid across boats or other structures.

9 *Transition* means passing from one state to another (from **trānseō**).

10 You would be expected to confirm the truth of the statement.

Language test SSB p. 49

1 **a** cum mīlitēs oppidum **cēpissent**, omnēs cīvēs maximē timēbant.
When the soldiers had captured the town, all the citizens were greatly afraid.

b cum dominus haec verba **dīxisset**, servī lībertīque dīligenter labōrāre coepērunt.
When the master had spoken these words, the slaves and freedmen began to work hard.

c lēgātus, cum centuriōnem ad sē **arcessīvisset**, eī praemium dedit.
When the commander had summoned the centurion to him, he gave him a reward.

d rēx et amīcī, cum ad aulam **pervēnissent**, cēnam splendidissimam cōnsūmpsērunt.
When the king and his friends had reached the palace, they ate a very splendid dinner.

e cum mīlitēs per urbem **quaererent**, fūr in silvā sē cēlābat.
When the soldiers were searching through the city, the thief was hiding (himself) in a wood.

f puerī, cum ad theātrum **contenderent**, multōs dēnāriōs in viā invēnērunt.
When the boys were hurrying to the theatre, they found a lot of money in the street.

2 **a** The horsemen, (having been) ordered to arrest the chieftain, carried out the orders immediately.

b You are a man of very great courage / a very brave man. Surely you wish to save the king and his friends?

c Have you heard the words of Salvius?

d We have too much work. Having been beaten by our master, we are unwilling to stay in this house.

e While walking in the king's garden, I caught sight of many very beautiful flowers.

f Everyone was looking at the lamb which had been led to the altar.

The two neuter nouns are **mandāta** and **verba**.

Revision

Pronouns II   p. 153

4 **a** illam   **e** huic   **h** id
b illōs   **f** eam   **i** eam
c hī   **g** eōs   **j** eius
d huius

Fourth and fifth declension nouns

Questions SSB p. 50

1 nominative singular; accusative singular.

2 accusative singular; nominative and accusative plural.

3 nominative and accusative plural.

4 **manus** (nominative singular) has a short **u**; **manūs** (nominative plural) has a long **ū**; therefore the pronunciation is different. See the pronunciation guide, SSB p. 108.

Para. 4   p. 147

a diēs   **d** manūs
b manum   **e** diēī
c genua

Dative case SSB p. 50

1 Finally they announced the matter to Salvius.

2 I trust neither Dumnorix nor Quintus.

3 It is easy for us to torture slaves.

4 Quintus is trying to obstruct a powerful man.

5 S/he cannot resist me.

6 He handed over the slave to the executioners.

7 Then he summoned a scribe to whom he dictated a letter.

In sentences 2, 4 and 5 the dative is due to the verbs **crēdō**, **obstāre** and **resistere**, which are followed by the dative case.

Stage 25 mīlitēs

Model sentences

Translation pp. 72–3

1   A soldier of the Second Legion was walking through the camp. Suddenly he caught sight of an unknown young man hiding near a granary.

'Hey you', shouted the soldier, 'who are you?'

The young man made no reply. The soldier asked the young man again who he was. The young man fled.

2   The soldier made for the young man and easily overpowered him.

'Scoundrel!' he exclaimed. 'What are you doing near the granary?'

The young man did not want to say what he was doing near the granary. The soldier led him to the centurion.

3   The centurion, having caught sight of the young man, said,

'I recognise this man! He is a British spy whom I've often caught sight of near the camp. How did you capture him?'

Then the soldier explained how he had captured the young man.

4   The centurion turned to the young man and asked,

'Why did you come into the camp?'

However, the young man was silent. When the centurion could not find out why the young man had come into camp, he ordered the soldier to take him to jail.

After the young man heard the words of the centurion, he said,

'I am Vercobrix, the son of the chieftain of the Deceangli. It is not right for you to hold me in jail.'

'The son of the chieftain of the Deceangli?' exclaimed the centurion. 'I'm very glad to see you. We have been looking for you for a long time, and we have prepared an excellent cell for you in jail.'

Questions SSB pp. 52–3

Sentences 1

a   Walking through the camp.

b   An unknown young man lurking near the granary.

c   **'quis es?'** *'Who are you?'*

d   He again asked the young man who he was.

e   The young man ran away.

Sentences 2

a   **'quid prope horreum facis?'** *'What are you doing near the granary?'*

b   The young man did not want to say **what he was doing near the granary.**

c   The soldier led him to the centurion.

Sentences 3

a   A British spy.

b   He had often seen him near the camp.

c   **'quō modō eum cēpistī?'** *'How did you catch him?'*

d   Then the soldier explained how he had caught the young man.

Sentences 4

a   **'cūr in castra vēnistī?'** *'Why did you come into the camp?'*

b   **tacēbat**.

c   The centurion, when **he was unable to find out why the young man had come into the camp**, ordered the soldier to take him to jail.

Last paragraph

a   When he heard the centurion's words / that he was to be taken to jail.

b   His name was Vercobrix. He was the son of the chieftain of the Deceangli.

c   He did not think it right for the Romans to keep him in prison.

d   They had been searching for him for a long time.

e   He is using **optimam** (*excellent*) sarcastically. The cell would probably be very uncomfortable and therefore excellent for the British spy.

Picture questions

1 The centurion's body armour consists of chain-mail; the soldier's has overlapping metal plates. The centurion's helmet has a plume, the soldier's is plain. The centurion has greaves (leg protections), the soldier does not. The centurion also has a cloak.

2 A vine-staff.

3 His spear/javelin and shield.

Strȳthiō SSB pp. 54–6

Option 1

Questions

1 At Deva (Chester).

2 He wishes to tell him something.

3 He tells the optio not to harass him as he is busy. He is looking for Modestus because a girl is waiting for him.

4 To hurry at once to the jail.

5 He considers the centurion to be mad and declares that he is innocent.

6 Modestus.

7 In lines 12–13, he is anxious to establish that he and Modestus are innocent of any wrong-doing. In lines 16–18, after hearing that the order is to guard the prison, he is relieved and jubilant and considers the centurion has made the right choice, since he and Modestus are very brave.

8 Diligence/carefulness.

9 When he and Modestus were serving in Africa, their job was to guard a whole province, not merely one man.

10

Lines	Dialogue	Tone
6–7	mī Strȳthiō, quamquam occupātissimus es, …	sarcastic/amused
10	tacē!	irritated
12	deōs testēs faciō. innocentēs sumus.	anxious/guilty
14	caudex! tacē!	frustrated/impatient
19	(*susurrāns*) difficile est mihi hoc crēdere.	incredulous/sarcastic/amused
20	quid dīcis?	suspicious/worried/enquiring (he wants the optio to speak louder)

Further work

1 a He catches sight of Strythio who has now returned to Chester.
   b I am looking for Modestus.
   c I make the gods my witnesses.
   d We have committed no crime.
   e I now understand the order.

The sentences do not contain a word in the nominative case and each sentence begins with an accusative.

2 a hūc venīte!
   b nōlīte mē vexāre!
   c tacēte!

Option 2

An optio is walking through the camp. He catches sight of Strythio who has now returned to Chester.

optio: Hey, Strythio! Come here! I want to tell you something.

Strythio: Don't bother me! I am busy. I am looking for Modestus, because a girl is waiting for him.

optio: The centurion orders you to hurry at once to the jail.

Strythio: The centurion is mad! I am innocent!

optio: Be quiet! The centurion has also ordered Modestus to hurry to the jail.

Strythio: I make the gods my witnesses! We have committed no crime!

optio: Blockhead! Shut up! The centurion has ordered both of you to guard the prison! Vercobrix is among the prisoners, a young man of great importance, whose father is chieftain of the Deceangli. You must guard Vercobrix very carefully.

Strythio: Don't be worried, my dear optio.
I now understand the situation.
Nothing is difficult for us, because we
are very brave.

They go out. The optio looks for the centurion, Strythio looks for his friend.

Picture questions

1 a A staff.
  b A wax tablet.
2 a Caecilius Avitus.
  b optio.
  c The Twentieth Legion.

Modestus custōs   SSB pp. 56–7

Question lines 1–6

Possibly Modestus is concerned about how to handle such an important prisoner / is afraid that he may be attacked by the prisoner.

Translation lines 7–20

Strythio said, 'Why are you afraid to enter the cell? The son of the chieftain of the Deceangli is tied up. He can't hurt you.' **When Strythio had said** these words, Modestus **angrily** exclaimed, 'Blockhead, **I am not afraid of** the son of the chieftain! I stopped because **I was waiting for you.** I want you **to open the door for me!' When** Strythio **had opened** the door, Modestus again **hesitated**.

'The cell is dark', said Modestus **anxiously**. 'Bring me a lamp.' Strythio, a very patient man, brought a lamp and handed it to his friend. He, **having entered** the cell, disappeared from sight.

Vercobrix was lying in the corner of the cell. Modestus, **when he had seen / saw him**, drew his sword. Then, **having gone forward to the middle of the cell**, he began to curse Vercobrix. However, Vercobrix could not hear the insults of Modestus because **he was in a deep sleep**.

Actions lines 21–3

	1st action	2nd action	3rd action
spider	dropped from ceiling	fell on Modestus' nose	ran across his face
Modestus	was frightened	fled from the cell	shouted loudly

Questions lines 24–end

1 He did not know why Modestus was shouting.
2 To shut the door of the cell, because they have to guard Vercobrix with the utmost care.
3 Not at all true, because only one spider is involved and it was not helping Vercobrix but just naturally dropping from the ceiling.
4 He does not want to admit that he is afraid of the prisoner and is on the defensive. His explanation for his paleness is that he has not eaten.
5 To go to the kitchen and fetch a meal for Modestus.
6 Strythio. The title is used in a sarcastic sense as it suggests that Modestus is the one guarding the jail, whereas he has done nothing but show fear and incompetence. Possible title changes might be **Modestus ignāvus / Modestus perterritus**, expressing his behaviour more accurately. You can probably think of other good titles.

Practising the language   p. 80

1 a Modestus et Strȳthiō, **cum carcerem intrāvissent**, cellās captīvōrum īnspiciēbant.
   When they had entered the prison, Modestus and Strythio began to inspect the cells of the prisoners.
  b **cum Modestus extrā cellam haesitāret**, Strȳthiō eum rogāvit cūr timēret.
   When Modestus was hesitating outside the cell, Strythio asked him why he was afraid.
  c Strȳthiō, **cum lucernam tulisset**, Modestō trādidit.
   When Strythio had brought the lamp, he handed it to Modestus.

d **cum Modestus vehementer clāmāret,**
Vercobrix graviter dormiēbat.
When Modestus was shouting loudly,
Vercobrix was sleeping soundly.

e **cum arānea in nāsum dēcidisset,**
Modestus fūgit perterritus.
When the spider had dropped on his nose,
Modestus fled in terror.

f **cum Modestus ad culīnam abiisset,**
Strȳthiō in carcere mānsit.
When Modestus had gone away to the
kitchen, Strythio remained in the prison.

About the language 1: indirect questions

Para. 4   p. 76

a 'Who killed the boy?'

b No one knew who had killed the boy.
interfēcisset: pluperfect subjunctive.

c 'Where did they find the money?'

d The judge asked me where they had found
the money.
invēnissent: pluperfect subjunctive.

e Salvius did not know why Quintus was
helping the king.
adiuvāret: imperfect subjunctive.

f Cogidubnus found out how Cephalus had
obtained the poison.
comparāvisset: pluperfect subjunctive.

g Quintus wanted to know what was in the
temple.
esset: imperfect subjunctive.

h Salvius at last understood where Quintus and
Dumnorix were fleeing to.
fugerent: imperfect subjunctive.

Further work SSB pp. 57–8

1 mīles explōrātōrem Britannicum rogāvit **cūr**
prope horreum stāret.
The soldier asked the British spy why he was
standing near the granary.
In bubble: 'Why are you standing near the
granary?'

2 mīles explōrātōrem rogāvit **quō modō castra**
Rōmāna intrāvisset.
The soldier asked the spy how he had entered the
Roman camp.
In bubble: 'How did you enter the Roman
camp?'

3 centuriō mīlitem rogāvit **ubi explōrātōrem**
Britannicum invēnisset.
The centurion asked the soldier where he had
found the British spy.
In bubble: 'Where did you find the British
spy?'

4 centuriō nōn cognōscere poterat **quid**
explōrātor in castrīs faceret.
The centurion was not able to find out what the
spy was doing in the camp.
In bubble: 'What are you doing in the camp?'

Modestus perfuga I   p. 77

SSB pp. 58–9

Translation

1 Having left the kitchen where he had eaten an
excellent meal, Modestus was returning slowly
to the prison.

2 When he drew near to the prison, he saw the
door open.
Modestus: **Good heavens! Strythio, surely**
you did not leave the door of the prison
open? I do not know anyone more careless
than you.

3 Having entered the prison, he found the doors
of all the cells open.
Modestus: **Alas! All the doors are open! The**
prisoners, having escaped from the cells,
have all fled!

4 Modestus anxiously considered the situation.
For he did not know where the prisoners had
fled; he could not understand why Strythio
was not there.
Modestus: **What ought I to do? It is dangerous**
to remain here where the centurion can find
me. I must flee. O Strythio, Strythio! You
have forced me to desert my post. You have
made me a deserter. But I make the gods my
witnesses. I desert my post against my will.

	Direct questions	Indirect questions
Latin	num portam carceris apertam relīquistī?	nesciēbat enim quō captīvī fūgissent.
Translation	Surely you did not leave the door of the prison open?	For he did not know where the prisoners had fled.
Latin	quid facere dēbeō?	intellegere nōn poterat cūr Strȳthiō abesset.
Translation	What ought I to do?	He could not understand why Strythio was absent.

Modestus perfuga II

Translation lines 1–11 p. 78 SSB p. 59

Having said these words, Modestus **suddenly heard a noise**. Someone was trying to open the door of Vercobrix's cell and escape!

'I must flee from jail', **someone called out from the cell**. Modestus, **when he had heard these words**, ran to the door of the cell and shut it.

'Vercobrix, you must remain in your cell!' shouted Modestus. 'Hurray! **Vercobrix has not escaped! I have him captive!** Hurray! Now the centurion cannot harm me because **I have kept in jail a prisoner of the greatest importance / a very important prisoner**.'

However, Modestus remained worried; for he did not know **what had happened** to Strythio. Suddenly he caught sight of **a dagger left on the ground**.

Translation lines 12–end p. 78

'Hey, what is it? I recognise this dagger! It is Strythio's dagger! I gave it to Strythio, when he was celebrating his birthday. Oh no! The dagger is covered in blood. O my dear Strythio! I now understand the truth. You are dead! The prisoners, having escaped from the cells, killed you. Oh dear!

When I was eating your dinner in the kitchen, they were fighting with you! O Strythio! No one is more unfortunate than I. For I loved you as a father loves his son. Vercobrix, who still remains in this cell, must pay the penalty. Hey! Vercobrix, listen to me! You must die, because my Strythio is dead.'

Modestus perfuga III SSB p. 60

1   In a rage Modestus burst into the cell and began beating up the prisoner cowering inside.

2   He assumed the prisoner was Vercobrix; it was in fact Strythio.

3   In saying **'num vīvus es?'** Modestus' tone would be one of incredulity and amazement. His next question **'cūr vīvus es?'** would reflect his indignation and disappointment.

4   'Where are the prisoners whom you were guarding?'

5   The prisoners had run away. They had deceived him and forced him to open the doors of all the cells.

6   They should flee from the prison at once, because he could hear the centurion approaching.

Further exercise

Part and line	Reaction	Reason
I. 3	permōtus	He was alarmed that the prison door was open; he may have felt guilty that he had been away.
I. 10	anxius	He was concerned that all the prisoners had gone and Strythio was also missing.
I. 15	invītus	He claimed to be reluctant to desert his post.
II. 7	euge!	He was overjoyed that his most important prisoner, Vercobrix, was still in his cell.
II. 10	anxius	He was worried about what had happened to Strythio.
II. 13	ēheu!	He was upset at finding Strythio's dagger covered in blood.
III. 1	furēns	He was enraged at Strythio's death.
III. 7	sceleste!	His grief for Strythio turned to anger when he found that Strythio had let all the prisoners escape, including Vercobrix.
III. 10	ēheu!	He was worried about how to escape punishment.
III. 13	ō, quam īnfēlīx sum!	He was lamenting that the centurion was about to arrive.

About the language 2: more about the imperfect and pluperfect subjunctive

Para. 3   p. 79   SSB p. 61

a   The guards asked us why we were shouting.
b   I did not know where you had fled.
c   When I was a soldier in Britain, I often visited the town of Bath.
d   When you were eating your dinner, the centurion was looking for you.
e   The king explained to us how you had saved his life.
f   When I had read out the names, I led the guests to the king.
g   My friend wanted to find out where you were living.
h   The girl asked us why we had undertaken so difficult a task.

	Subjunctive	1st singular	1st plural	2nd singular	2nd plural	Imperfect	Pluperfect
a	clāmārēmus		✓			✓	
b	fūgissēs			✓			✓
c	mīlitārem	✓				✓	
d	cōnsūmerēs			✓		✓	
e	servāvissētis				✓		✓
f	recitāvissem	✓					✓
g	habitārētis				✓	✓	
h	suscēpissēmus		✓				✓

Further work SSB p. 61

1   The imperfect subjunctive can be recognised because it is formed from the infinitive with the personal ending added, e.g. **clāmāre-mus** (**clāmārēmus**).

The pluperfect subjunctive can be recognised because it has **-isse-** before the personal ending, e.g. **servāv-issē-tis** (**servāvissētis**).

The imperfect and pluperfect subjunctive of irregular verbs are formed in the same way, e.g. imperfect subjunctive **posse-t** (**posset**), pluperfect subjunctive **volu-issē-mus** (**voluissēmus**).

2   audīrētis; portārēmus; mitterent; mīsissent; timērēmus; laudāvissētis; dūxissēmus; essent.

Word patterns: male and female

Paras 1–3   p. 80

1 | male | female |
| --- | --- |
| dominus | domina |
| leō | leaena |
| deus | dea |
| fīlius | fīlia |
| captīvus | captīva |

2 | saltātor | saltātrīx |
| --- | --- |
| vēnātor | vēnātrīx |
| avus | avia |
| victor | victrīx |
| ursus | ursa |
| lupus | lupa |

3   The endings **-us** (usually) and **-tor** indicate masculine nouns. The endings **-a** (usually) and **-trīx** indicate feminine nouns.

Further work SSB p. 62

1   rēx, rēgīna

2   In paragraph 1: mistress; lioness; goddess.
In paragraph 2: huntress.
Some other examples are: princess; duchess; waitress.

Practising the language continued

p. 81   SSB p. 62

2   a   captīvī, ē cellīs subitō **līberātī**, ad portam carceris ruērunt.
The prisoners, suddenly freed from their cells, rushed to the door of the prison.

b   Britannī, hastās in manibus **tenentēs**, castra oppugnāvērunt.
The Britons, holding spears in their hands, attacked the camp.

c   ancilla, ā dominō īrātō **territa**, respondēre nōn audēbat.
The slave-girl, frightened by her angry master, did not dare to reply.

d   Cogidubnus, tot iniūriās **passus**, Rōmānōs vehementer vituperāvit.
Cogidubnus, having suffered so many injustices, loudly cursed the Romans.

e   māter puellam, ē tabernā tandem **regressam**, pūnīvit.
The mother punished the girl, who had at last returned from the shop.

f   centuriō mīlitēs, ex Ītaliā nūper ab Imperātōre **missōs**, īnspexit.
The centurion inspected the soldiers, recently sent from Italy by the emperor.

	Noun	Participle	Case	Number	Gender
a	captīvī	līberātī	nominative	plural	masculine
b	Britannī	tenentēs	nominative	plural	masculine
c	ancilla	territa	nominative	singular	feminine
d	Cogidubnus	passus	nominative	singular	masculine
e	puellam	regressam	accusative	singular	feminine
f	mīlitēs	missōs	accusative	plural	masculine

3   a   cīvēs benignī auxilium praebuerant.

    b   mīlitem in culīnā tabernae comprehendērunt.

    c   domine! hanc epistulam lege!

    d   verba haruspicis eum terruērunt.

    e   senēs discessērunt, fortem nūntium laudantēs.

    f   quō modō poenās deōrum vītāre possumus?

The legionary soldier SSB pp. 63–4

1   a   The javelin (**pīlum**). When it was thrown from a distance the specially tempered head stuck in the enemy's shield, while the shaft hung down. The enemy could neither re-use the pilum nor manage his now-encumbered shield. The legionaries stood a good chance of killing or disabling some of the enemy at a distance without endangering themselves.

    b   They would cause fear because of their massed close ranks with their huge shields and the frightening devices on them, as well as the array of short swords ready for attack.

2   An officer (left) wearing a moulded breast plate and military cloak; legionaries, with breast plates of overlapping plates; a standard-bearer (right) wearing a bearskin.

3   a   The kit would contain tools such as an axe and saw and a basket for moving soil.

    b   The legionaries have put their shields against a wall and then rested their helmets on top of the shields.
    The auxiliaries are on guard duty but seem to be rather relaxed and enjoying a chat.

4   a   Examples of specialised troops in a modern army are the SAS, tank units, drivers, engineers.

    b   The auxiliaries would have been provided with food and accommodation; they had the prestige of being attached to the legionaries; they might enjoy travel and varied experiences, and they were granted Roman citizenship at the end of their service.

5   The success of the Roman army was due to:
Scrupulous recruitment: recruits had to be of a high standard.
Excellent training: long weapon practice, forced marches, camp building.
Good discipline: enforced by the centurions, noted for their strictness.
Good health: the army usually had adequate rations, good sanitation in the camps and a competent medical service.
High morale: resulting from its professionalism and superiority over most of its less well trained opponents.

Possible difficulties for the Roman army were:
Being caught in a position where their normal troop formation was at a disadvantage, e.g. in a forest.
Fighting against guerrillas.
Losing their cavalry in the early stage of a battle.

6   a   tesserārius

    b   cornicen

    c   centuriō

    d   aquilifer

    e   signifer

    f   praefectus castrōrum

    g   lēgātus

    h   optiō

Vocabulary checklist 25 SSB p. 64

1   A happening, without blame attached to anyone.

2   The opening which controls the light (from **aperiō**).

3   Forceful (from **cōgō**).

4   You are putting your trust in someone.

5   A mistake which cannot be explained (from **explicō**, combined with negative 'in-').

6   They take place outside the normal timetable.

7   *Nominal* means existing in name only, i.e. of very little value or cost.

8   I should not be pleased as I would be going to receive punishment. *Penal* is from **poena** (*penalty* or *punishment*).

Language test SSB p. 65

1. a cum cēnārem
   b cum mīlitārēmus
   c cum clausisset
   d cum vīdissent
   e cum haesitārēs

2. a Modestus did not know where the prisoners had fled.
   b He was not able to understand why Strythio was absent.
   c Modestus asked him in which cell Vercobrix was lying.
   d He did not know why Modestus had shouted.
   e He asked the terrified Modestus what had happened.
   f The centurion wanted to know where you were.
   g Modestus could not find out who had opened the door of the prison.
   h I told the optio how we had guarded the whole province.

Revision

Participles

Para. 4 p. 161

a The slave-girls, **working** in the house, did not see the thief.
b The slave, **having been ordered** by the freedman, prepared the poison.
c The woman, **having caught sight** of her husband, quickly hid the money.
d The soldiers set fire to the city **which had been captured**.
e Modestus was not able to find the prisoners, **after they had gone out** from the prison.
f Salvius was standing in the headquarters, **raging**.

	Participle	Description	Noun
a	labōrantēs	present	ancillae
b	iussus	perfect passive	servus
c	cōnspicāta	perfect active	fēmina
d	captam	perfect passive	urbem
e	ēgressōs	perfect active	captīvōs
f	saeviēns	present	Salvius

Further exercise **SSB p. 66**

a puellae, in culīnā **labōrantēs**, garriēbant.
   The girls, working in the kitchen, were chattering.
b soror Vilbiae, fībulam **cōnspicāta**, īnspicere volēbat.
   Vilbia's sister, having caught sight of the brooch, wanted to inspect it.
c mīlitēs lēgātum **appropinquantem** vīdērunt.
   The soldiers saw the commander approaching.
d Vilbia, ā Modestō **arcessīta**, thermās intrāvit.
   Vilbia, summoned by Modestus, entered the baths.
e centuriō Modestum et Strȳthiōnem, ad castra **regressōs**, carcerem custōdīre iussit.
   The centurion ordered Modestus and Strythio, having returned to the camp / after they had returned to the camp, to guard the prison.

	Noun and participle pair	Case	Number	Gender
a	puellae … labōrantēs	nominative	plural	feminine
b	soror … cōnspicāta	nominative	singular	feminine
c	lēgātum appropinquantem	accusative	singular	masculine
d	Vilbia … arcessīta	nominative	singular	feminine
e	Modestum et Strȳthiōnem … regressōs	accusative	plural	masculine

Para. 7 **p. 162**

a   trahentēs

b   portātae

c   ingressus

Irregular verbs

Para. 2 **p. 159**

you (s.) are able; s/he wants; I am going; s/he goes; you (s.) bring.

to be able; I have been; s/he was going; they were taking; we brought.

you (pl.) took; we had been; you (pl.) went; they had been able; they were able / they could.

Further examples **SSB p. 66**

you (s.) want; s/he was returning; you (s.) took; s/he brought; you (s.) are; s/he was not able; they are doing; to want; I was fleeing; when s/he was absent.

Stage 26 Agricola

adventus Agricolae SSB p. 68–9

1 The Second Legion.
2 Gaius Iulius Silanus, the commander of the legion, was waiting for the arrival of Agricola.
3 Polishing armour; cleaning buildings; repairing carts.
4 The soldiers, **unaware of Agricola's arrival**, were taking the situation badly. They worked for three days on end; **on the fourth day** Silanus announced the arrival of Agricola. The soldiers, **when they (had) heard this**, were extremely pleased because they liked Agricola.
5 In order that / so that they might greet Agricola.
6 In order that / so that he might say a few things (words).
7 In order that / so that they might hear Agricola.
8 a A personal touch – Agricola sounded warm and human, as though he were greeting old friends.
   b He was praising them for their loyalty and courage, making them seem special and appreciated.
   c He was praising their professionalism and keenness; he showed he had noticed the efforts they had made.
9 Having encouraged the soldiers in this way, he proceeded along the lines *in order that / so that he might inspect them*. Then he entered the headquarters *in order that / so that he might have a conversation with Silanus*.
10 a iii A purpose or intention.
    b It is the imperfect subjunctive.

How we know about Agricola

SSB pp. 69–70

1 By stating when certain people were in office. Here, the inscription is dated by the consulship of Vespasian and Titus, i.e. AD 79.
2 If we know that the lines in question are likely to refer only to names and titles, we can supply the missing words from our existing knowledge of other official inscriptions.

Picture question

1 Silanus, commander of the legion / **lēgātus legiōnis**.
2 Agricola, governor of Britain, commander in chief.
3 Centurions/**centuriōnēs**.
4 Eagle-bearer/**aquilifer**.
5 Standard-bearer/**signifer**.

in prīncipiīs

Questions   p. 93

		Marks
1	Salvius was waiting (anxiously) for Agricola.	1
2	Salvius was worried because he had told many lies in the letter he had sent to Agricola.	2
3	He had accused Cogidubnus of rebellion.	1
4	He had brought Belimicus with him to be a witness.	1
5	He was probably shocked to hear the accusations from Salvius in person / He might have been trying to keep calm / He found the accusations almost incomprehensible.	1
6	Agricola ends by believing Salvius. He says they ought never to trust barbarians / He says the barbarians always betrayed them.	1
7	Agricola told Silanus they must crush the king and the chieftains of the Regnenses as quickly as possible. Silanus must set out at once with two cohorts.	2 + 1

8   Agricola tried to find out more about
    Cogidubnus' treachery.   1

9   Salvius said that Belimicus' character
    was excellent and that he was extremely
    trustworthy. He had told Salvius
    everything about Cogidubnus' attempt
    to corrupt him.   2 + 2

10 Agricola might or might not have
    believed that Cogidubnus hated the
    Romans / wanted to drive the Romans
    from Britain / take over the whole island
    / was obtaining ships / was training
    soldiers / was collecting wild beasts /
    had driven a wild beast at him in order
    to kill him. *(It is, however, unlikely that
    Agricola would have believed the last two
    accusations.) Give two marks for two points.*   2

11 Agricola wanted to find out how many
    armed men there were, whether the
    Britons had killed Roman citizens, which
    cities they had destroyed.   3

12 The accusations against Cogidubnus
    were false and Salvius would have found
    it difficult to answer detailed questions
    about them.   1

13 A man, covered in dirt, burst through
    the door of the principia.   1

14 He ran headlong to Agricola and clung
    to his knees.   2

15 **multās iniūriās passus**.   1
                                          ——
                                    TOTAL 25

Further questions SSB p. 71

1   Salvius had previously sent Belimicus to hunt
    down Quintus and Dumnorix. He could not
    find out very quickly whether Belimicus was
    successful or not. He therefore decided to
    see Agricola in person before Quintus could
    incriminate him.

2   Agricola felt betrayed by Cogidubnus. He
    thought Cogidubnus was an ally, but now
    he has been told that he was a traitor to the
    Romans.

3   No. Belimicus overstated the case against

Cogidubnus, with the far-fetched accusations
about Cogidubnus collecting wild animals
and trying to kill Belimicus with one. This
might have made Agricola sceptical about all
the other accusations against Cogidubnus.

4   To establish his status. As a Roman citizen,
    Quintus could rely on being heard by
    Agricola. He might otherwise have been
    disbelieved, or even killed outright. By giving
    his full name, Quintus reinforced the fact that
    he was a Roman citizen.

5   **A** *Character*: Agricola.
        Adjective: efficient.
        Reason: He acts very quickly in sending
        Silanus to deal with the (alleged) revolt
        of Cogidubnus and the chieftains of the
        Regnenses and to find out the facts.
        Or,
        Adjective: shrewd.
        Reason: He does not believe Belimicus'
        wild accusations and orders Silanus to
        collect hard evidence.

    B *Character*: Salvius.
        Adjective: anxious.
        Reason: He was worried because his
        accusations were based on lies.

    C *Character*: Belimicus.
        Adjective: unintelligent.
        Reason: His accusations were overstated
        and immediately raised doubts in
        Agricola's mind.

    D *Character*: Quintus.
        Adjective: exhausted.
        Reason: He had been seriously wounded
        in the fight with Belimicus and the
        cavalry and had made his way to Chester
        with great difficulty. He collapsed when
        he reached Agricola.
        Or,
        Adjective: brave.
        Reason: Despite his wounds and the
        danger of the journey, he courageously
        struggled on alone to Chester.

About the language 1: purpose clauses p. 94 SSB p. 72

2

a All the citizens hurried to the wood in order that they might look at the dead lion.

b The master demanded a pen and wax tablets in order that he might write a letter.

c Finally I returned to my father in order that I might explain the matter.

d I seized a dagger in order that I might kill the prisoner.

e We quickly mounted horses in order that we might escape from the town.

f You entered the house in order that you might take our money.

You may have translated the purpose clauses correctly in a different way, e.g.:

a All the citizens hurried to the wood to / in order to look at the dead lion. (See paragraph 3.)

3

a Suddenly Salvius hurried towards him to / in order to greet him.

b Recently he pushed a wild animal towards me to / in order to kill me.

tribūnus SSB pp. 72–3

1 'I can explain everything.' Salvius was very alarmed (**valdē commōtus**), because Quintus had arrived and would give a different version of events. He probably spoke in a hasty, unconvincing way.

3 Agricola was cautious and said 'If *he has done these things, he should die*'.

4 Rufus thought Quintus was a very reliable young man, whereas Salvius said he was more treacherous than the Britons.

5 Rufus' father knew Quintus well, and Rufus had his father's letter to prove it.

6 Barbillus, the wealthy Alexandrian business man.

7 Quintus now had the chance to talk to Agricola in private.

8 **mox revēnit Rūfus valdē attonitus** (line 19). *Soon Rufus returned, greatly astonished.*
Or, **'hoc prō certō ... scrīptam'** (lines 21–3). *'I know this for certain, because Quintus has shown me this letter, written by my father himself.'*

The senior officers in the Roman army SSB p. 73

Although most senior officers frequently came and went, the centurions ensured that the legions were efficiently run. The centurions who had been in the legions as young soldiers themselves and had worked their way up through the ranks, had huge experience. Also, they provided the army with such a strong tradition of training and discipline that the army could be relied on to be successful, even if its officers were relatively inexperienced.

2

Line	Accusation	T/F	Reason/Comment
9	nūper ... nōn invītāveram	T	Strictly speaking true. It was his wife Rufilla who invited Quintus, but Salvius implies that Quintus came uninvited.
9–10	trēs ... dēvorāns	F	There is no evidence that Quintus devoured Salvius' wealth; he was a courteous guest.
10–12	duōs ... erat	F	The two silver tripods given to Cogidubnus were Quintus' own.
12–15	ubi ... accūsāvit	F	Quintus did not attempt to poison Memor and then accuse Salvius; in fact Salvius ordered Memor to find a way to murder Cogidubnus.

About the language 2: gerundives SSB p. 73

1–2 The case of the words is dative.

3 a I must **run away**.

   b **We** must walk.

   c **You (s.) must** wait here.

   d The slaves **must** work **carefully**.

   e All the **citizens must** be silent because the priests **are approaching**.

   f If they want to see the **emperor, they must hurry**.

contentiō

Option 1 Students working on their own
SSB p. 74

Summary of Agricola's speech

1 Cogidubnus is innocent, you (are) treacherous.

2 My friends warned me about your cunning.

3 Surely the Emperor Domitian cannot tolerate/bear such (great) treachery as this?

4 In this province I have the highest power.

5 I order you to go to Cogidubnus' palace, and to seek pardon from him.

6 Besides, you ought to explain the matter to the emperor himself.

Summary of Salvius' speech

1 How blind you are! What a big mistake you are making / How greatly mistaken you are!

2 You bring back meaningless victories from Scotland.

3 The emperor wants to receive money and wealth.

4 And so he has decided to seize Cogidubnus' kingdom.

5 You are in great danger because you reject my plan.

6 You are obstructing not only me but the emperor himself.

Option 2 Students working in groups p. 97

Translation of Agricola's speech lines 4–11

'Good heavens! Cogidubnus is innocent, you (are) treacherous. Why was I so mad that I trusted you?

As soon as you came to this province, my friends warned me about your cunning. Now the event itself has taught me. Surely the Emperor Domitian cannot tolerate/bear such treachery as this? I certainly can't. In this province I have the highest power. I order you to lay aside these feuds. I order you to go to Cogidubnus' palace, and to seek pardon from him. Besides, you ought to explain the matter to the emperor himself.'

Translation of Salvius' speech lines 13–19

'How blind you are! What a big mistake you are making / How greatly mistaken you are! You yourself ought to explain to the emperor what you are doing in Britain. For you are waging war in the furthest parts of Britain and you bring back meaningless victories from Scotland; but the emperor wants to receive money and wealth. And so he has decided to seize Cogidubnus' kingdom; he does not care about Scotland. You certainly don't know this. You are in great danger, because you reject my plan. You are obstructing not only me but the emperor himself.'

Question for everyone SSB p. 74

A messenger suddenly rushed in with news that Cogidubnus was dead.

Further work SSB p. 75

1 a *Suggested sentence for Agricola:*
      'in hāc prōvinciā summam potestātem habeō.'
      Suggested sentence for Salvius:
      'nōn sōlum mihi sed Imperātōrī ipsī obstās.'
      Or, 'Imperātor rēgnum Cogidubnī occupāre cōnstituit.'

   b Agricola will win the power struggle because he is of higher status than Salvius.
      Or, Salvius will win because he is acting under orders from Domitian himself.

2 Quintus handed over the letter to Rufus. When he/Rufus had read it, he was very amazed.

Word patterns: verbs and nouns

Para. 3 p. 98

verbs		nouns	
timēre	*to fear*	timor	*fear*
dolēre	(1) *to hurt, to be in pain*	dolor	(1) *pain*
dolēre	(2) *to grieve*	dolor	(2) *grief*
favēre	*to favour*	favor	*favour*
furere	*to be in a rage*	furor	*rage*
labōrāre	*to work*	labor	*work*

Further work SSB p. 75

Latin and English nouns: **horror, error, ardor, pallor**.

Practising the language p. 99

SSB p. 76

1   a   Agricola, ubi verba **Quīntī** audīvit, Salvium arcessīvit.
       Agricola, when he heard Quintus' words, summoned Salvius.

   b   omnēs hospitēs **artem** saltātrīcis laudāvērunt.
       All the guests praised the skill of the dancing-girl.

   c   iter nostrum difficile erat, quod tot cīvēs **viās** complēbant.
       Our journey was difficult, because so many citizens were filling the streets.

   d   prō prīncipiīs stābat magna turba **mīlitum**.
       In front of the headquarters was standing a large crowd of soldiers.

   e   lēgātus, postquam mandāta **centuriōnibus** dedit, legiōnem ad montem proximum dūxit.
       The commander, after he gave instructions to the centurions, led the legion to the nearest mountain.

   f   iūdex, quī **puerīs** nōn crēdēbat, īrātissimus erat.
       The judge, who did not believe the boys, was very angry.

2   a   cum Sīlānus legiōnem **īnstrūxisset**, Agricola ē prīncipiīs prōcessit.
       When Silanus had drawn up the legion, Agricola made his way out of the headquarters.

   b   mīlitēs in flūmen dēsiluērunt ut hostēs **vītārent**.
       The soldiers jumped down into the river to avoid the enemy.

   c   senātor scīre voluit num pater meus Imperātōrī **fāvisset**.
       The senator wanted to know whether my father had supported the emperor.

   d   cum senex **dormīret**, fūrēs per fenestram tacitē intrāvērunt.
       When the old man was sleeping, thieves silently entered through the window.

   e   nōs, cum in Britanniā **essēmus**, barbarōs saepe vīcimus.
       When we were in Britain, we often defeated the barbarians.

   f   intellegere nōn poteram cūr cīvēs istum hominem **laudāvissent**.
       I could not understand why the citizens had praised that man.

   g   latrōnem interfēcī ut īnfantem **servārem**.
       I killed the robber to save the baby.

   h   māter tua mē rogāvit quid in tabernā **fēcissēs**.
       Your mother asked me what you had done in the pub.

Containing purpose clauses
Sentences: **b** and **g**
Introductory word: **ut**

Containing indirect questions
Sentences: **c, f** and **h**
Introductory words: **num, cūr** and **quid**

3   a   Salvius, ē prīncipiīs **ēgressus**, Belimicum quaesīvit.
       Having gone out of the headquarters, Salvius looked for Belimicus.

b Agricola, cum haec verba **audīvisset**, ad Rūfum sē vertit.

When Agricola had heard these words, he turned to Rufus.

c dominus **epistulam** ē manibus servī furēns rapuit.

The master furiously snatched the letter from the hands of the slave.

d custōdēs nūntium sub aquā iacentem **invēnērunt**.

The guards found the messenger lying beneath the water.

e quattuor Britannī, in pugnā **captī**, vītam dūrissimam in carcere agēbant.

Four Britons, captured in battle, were spending a very harsh life in prison.

f aliī mīlitēs **equīs** aquam dabant, aliī frūmentum in horrea īnferēbant.

Some soldiers were giving water to the horses, others were bringing grain into the granaries.

Agricola, governor of Britain

SSB pp. 76–7

1

a His 'passionate interest' was in philosophy.

b The situation referred to is the revolt of Boudica in AD 60.

c It would help his policy to romanise the British.

d Mons Graupius was in Scotland in the Grampian mountains where Agricola won a great victory. No one knows the exact site of the battle; for one possibility see the map on p. 139.

2 Agricola spent an unusually long time as governor in Britain, seven years.

Picture question

The Caledonians would probably have felt humiliated and resentful at the way they were depicted, trampled by the Roman cavalryman. They might also feel powerless in the face of the superior force of the Romans.

Vocabulary checklist 26 SSB p. 77

1 **b.** A *belligerent* person behaves aggressively (from **bellum** and **gerō**).

2 People who are excited or upset sometimes cause a *commotion*.

3 **docēre** means *to teach*. A *docile* dog is calm, easy to manage and teachable.

4 *Fido* comes from **fidēs**, so it is a good name for a dog because it suggests loyalty.

5 The rail company set a *quota*, i.e. stated how many children could travel free of charge.

6 The athlete's *ultimate* ambition was to win an Olympic gold medal.

7 The *penultimate* page of the book was cut out (from **paene** *almost* and **ultimus** *last*).

8 I was *referred* to the library.

9 He enjoyed *relating* the story. (**referō, referre, rettulī, relātus.**)

10 I took away; I had taken away; they draw up; they drew up; we were offering; you (s.) offered.

Language test SSB p. 78

1

a lēgātus mīlitēs īnstrūxit **ut Agricola eōs īnspiceret.**

*The commander drew up the soldiers **so that Agricola might inspect them**.*

b Agricola Quīntum ad sē vocāvit **ut colloquium habēret.**

*Agricola called Quintus to him **to have a conversation**.*

c omnia Agricolae nārrāvī **ut mihi crēderet.**

*I told everything to Agricola **so that he would believe me**.*

d mīles ad castra festīnāvit **ut mortem Cogidubnī nūntiāret.**

*A soldier hurried to the camp **to announce the death of Cogidubnus**.*

e diū manēbāmus **ut vērum cognōscerēmus.**

*We stayed for a long time **to find out the truth**.*

f mē vīsitāvistī **ut pecūniam meam auferrēs.**

*You visited me **in order to steal my money**.*

2 **a** The soldiers ought to hurry.

    b The prisoners must not escape.

    c You (pl.) must run as fast as possible.

    d The guards must not sleep in the prison.

    e If the emperor is present, everyone must be quiet.

Revision

ipse

Question **SSB p. 78**

The genitive and dative singular of **ipse** are like those of **is**, **ea**, **id** *he*, *she*, *it*.

Further examples p. 154

a I myself saw the fight.

b We ourselves were present in the temple.

c Suddenly we heard the king himself.

d The goddess herself appeared to me.

Word order p. 165 SSB p. 78

1 **a** Modestus ran away.

    b The merchants returned.

2 **a** The thieves seized the money.

    b Agricola was inspecting the soldiers.

3 **a** Cephalus was holding a wine-cup.

    b The citizens set up a statue.

4 **a** The messenger departed.
      Nominative: last.

    b The enemy made an attack.
      Nominative: second.

    c The craftsman repaired the wall.
      Nominative: last.

    d The prisoner demanded water.
      Nominative: second.

    e The boys were annoying me.
      Nominative: last.

    f The babies perished.
      Nominative: last.

The sentences still make sense because the endings of the words in Latin indicate the role they play in the sentence.

5 **a** In this city.

    b With many soldiers.

    c To the small town.

    d With all the legions.

    e Through the whole night.

    f In the middle of the river.

More about word order **SSB p. 79**

1 When Modestus was standing in the cell, a spider fell on him.
Word emphasised: **arānea**.
Effect intended: to leave the reader in suspense until the last word to find out what fell on Modestus. Here the word order is used for comic effect. To get the same effect in English is not easy. Perhaps 'When Modestus was standing in the cell, there fell on him a spider'. Compare the rhyme about Miss Muffet: 'There came a big spider and sat down beside her.'

2 The goddess has sent excellent omens to us.
Word emphasised: **optima**.
Effect intended: to convey immediately the good news of the goddess' favour. In English one would have to say something like 'Excellent are the omens that the goddess has sent to us'.

Pronouns III: quī

Question **SSB p. 80**

All the pronouns on pp. 153–4 have:

-ius in genitive singular, masculine, feminine and neuter.

-i or **-ī** in dative singular, masculine, feminine and neuter.

Further examples p. 155

1 **a** The soldiers, **whom** Salvius sent out, eventually returned.

    b The young man, **whose** father was away in Greece, invited his friends to a lavish dinner.

    c The father very severely punished his daughters, **who** had met (with) the soldiers in the town.

    d The slave, **to whom** the priest had given a signal, led the two victims to the altar.

    e I often used to visit the temple, **which** stood in the middle of the city.

    f I quickly read the letter, **which** the messenger had brought.

Table **SSB p. 80**

	Noun	Relative pronoun	Case of relative pronoun	Number of relative pronoun	Gender of relative pronoun
a	mīlitēs	quōs	accusative	plural	masculine
b	iuvenis	cuius	genitive	singular	masculine
c	fīliās	quae	nominative	plural	feminine
d	servus	cui	dative	singular	masculine
e	templum	quod	nominative	singular	neuter
f	epistulam	quam	accusative	singular	feminine

Stage 27 in castrīs

Model sentences SSB pp. 82–3

Questions

Sentences 1

a 'Run away with me to the granary!'

b **anxiī** *worried.*
   (Complete translation of sentence: *Modestus and Strythio were anxiously having a conversation.*)

c Modestus was advising Strythio **to run away with him to the granary**.

Sentences 2

a 'Find Modestus and Strythio!'

b In front of the headquarters.
   (Complete translation: *The centurion was giving orders to the soldiers in front of the headquarters.*)

c The centurion was ordering the soldiers **to find Modestus and Strythio**.

Sentences 3

a 'Attack the Roman camp! Burn the granaries!'

b In a nearby wood.
   (Complete translation: *In a nearby wood Vercobrix was making a speech to* (lit. *among*) *the Britons.*)

c Vercobrix was urging the Britons **to attack the Roman camp and burn the granaries**.

Further questions

1 monēre   *to advise*
   imperāre   *to order*
   incitāre   *to urge on / encourage*
   ut follows each of these verbs.

2 **Differences between the Roman and British troops**

Romans	British
They are drawn up in an orderly line.	They stand around their leader in no particular order.
They look highly disciplined.	They are in informal groups.
The Romans wear standard battle armour, every piece of which has been carefully designed, e.g. the helmet with its neck-guard.	Their clothing and shields are not standardised; their lack of body armour and inferior helmets make them look vulnerable.
The centurion wears distinctive armour, which would identify him to his troops in battle.	Their leader does not stand out, unless his plaid cloak is meant to distinguish him from his men.

Granaries SSB p. 83

1 The floors are raised on wooden supports or low walls to allow the air to circulate and to keep vermin at bay. Later granaries had stone walls to the ground, but inside the floors were still raised on stone supports (see p. 117).

2 a The roof had wide overhanging eaves to carry the rain-water away from the walls.

   b Granaries could store enough for one or possibly two years.

in horreō SSB pp. 83–4

1 Any three expressions from the paragraph:
   quam īnfēlīx sum!
   How unlucky I am!
   mālim in illō carcere esse potius quam in hōc horreō latēre.
   I should prefer to be in that prison rather than lie hidden in this granary.
   ēheu!
   Oh dear!
   quālis est haec vīta?
   What sort of life is this?

2 The grain would not be edible as it had not been ground into flour or cooked.

3 Strythio offers to leave the granary and go and look for food.

4 He says food always brings hope to men who are very miserable.

5   'We must eat / have a dinner.'
6   Aulus   A   coquus   D
    Nigrina   B   Publicus   C
7   Nigrina.
8   A woman would be very conspicuous in a camp full of Roman soldiers and would not have been allowed anyway. She may also think that a party in a granary with Modestus is not worth the risk.

About the language 1: indirect commands

Para. 3   SSB p. 84

a   centuriō mīlitibus imperāvit ut Modestum et Strȳthiōnem caperent.
    The centurion ordered the soldiers **to capture Modestus and Strythio.**
    Direct command: 'Capture Modestus and Strythio.'

b   Strȳthiō coquō persuāsit ut cēnam splendidam parāret.
    Strythio persuaded the cook **to prepare a splendid dinner.**
    Direct command: 'Prepare a splendid dinner.'

c   Nigrīnam ōrāvit ut in castra venīret.
    He begged Nigrina **to come into the camp.**
    Direct command: 'Come into the camp.'

Para. 4   p. 109

a   'Be quiet!'
b   The centurion ordered me to be quiet.
c   'Spare me!'
d   The old man was begging us to spare him.
e   No one was able to persuade the slave-girl to dance.
f   The cook ordered the slaves to put the wine on the table.
g   I often used to advise you to work hard.
h   The soldiers warned the merchant to leave the town quickly.

Modestus prōmōtus I

Translation lines 1–11   p. 109   SSB p.85

When Strythio **was looking for** dinner and his friends, ten Britons, **(having been) led by Vercobrix**, were cautiously approaching the camp. For Vercobrix **had persuaded them** to attack the camp. After the Britons avoided the guards, they **entered the camp**. They were holding torches in their hands **to burn the granaries**. They reached the granaries quickly because earlier **they had found out** where **they were situated**. Modestus, **unaware of the arrival of the Britons**, was sitting in the granary. He was so hungry **that he almost despaired for his life**. He was looking out through the opening, **waiting for the return of Strythio**. 'I've already been waiting for **Strythio for three hours**. What **has happened to him**?' Suddenly **he caught sight of** a band of men **through the darkness**.

Questions lines 12–24   SSB p. 85

1   *Modestus* called out 'Friends, come over here!'
2   *The Britons* (**Britannī**), in amazement, didn't dare to reply.
3   *Vercobrix* made an insulting remark about Modestus and said he was harmless.
4   *A certain Briton* (**Britannus quīdam**) bumped into Modestus and was mistaken for Nigrina.
5   *Modestus* asked who had the lamp.

Translation lines 25–end   p. 110

When Vercobrix (had) heard Modestus asking for the lamp, he ordered the Britons to light their torches. Modestus, having caught sight of Vercobrix and the Britons, went pale.

'Good heavens!' he said. 'Nigrina has gone (away), the Britons have appeared! I must escape immediately.'

Further work   SSB p. 85

1   Lines 2–3: Vercobrix enim eīs persuāserat **ut castra oppugnārent.**
    Line 26: Britannīs imperāvit **ut facēs incenderent.**

2   in manibus *in their hands*
    manum hominum *a band of men*

Modestus prōmōtus II

Questions p. 111

Marks

1   Vercobrix ordered his men to seize
    Modestus.   1

2   One of the Britons approached Modestus
    to tie him up. However, the torch he was
    holding accidentally set fire to Modestus'
    tunic.   3

3   Modestus had snatched the amphora of
    wine from Aulus and poured it on his
    tunic / Modestus had rushed on fire
    from the granary (and Strythio could
    not understand this).   2

4   **(Modestus) ... Strȳthiōnis clāmōrum
    neglegēns.** *(Modestus) taking no notice
    of Strythio's shouts.*   2

5   He forced it into the entrance.   1

6   He claimed to have captured the Britons.   1

7   They wanted to find out the reason for
    the din.   1

8   The number of the Romans was so great
    that they easily overcame the Britons.   2

9   The Romans dragged them out of the
    granary and led them back to prison.   2

10 He said he had never before seen a braver
    soldier than Modestus / 'Modestus, I
    have never before seen a braver soldier
    than you.'   2

11 Modestus expected money. He was put in
    charge of the prison.   2

12 *No.* Modestus had shown that he was
    incompetent as a guard / He was too
    much of a coward to be any use.
    Yes. He did not deserve any better
    reward / It was in fact a fitting
    punishment for him / The reader who,
    unlike the legatus, knows the whole story,
    may think it a suitable reward for Modestus. 1

TOTAL 20

Table SSB p. 86

	Statement	T/F	Reason if false
1	Modestus prepared an ambush for the Britons.	F	He only claimed he had.
2	There was a brief struggle.	T	
3	Modestus and his friends easily overpowered the Britons.	F	The large number of Roman soldiers did.
4	Then Modestus summoned the commander.	F	The commander summoned Modestus.
5	Modestus was so pleased that he could hardly contain himself.	T	
6	Modestus was delighted when he received money as a reward.	F	He was pleased at the thought of a money reward. Actually his reward was to be put in charge of the prison.

About the language 2: result clauses

Translations para. 1 SSB p. 86

1   Modestus adeō ēsuriēbat ut dē vītā paene
    dēspērāret.
    *Modestus was so hungry **that he almost
    despaired of his life**.*

2   Britannī erant tam attonitī ut immōtī stārent.
    *The Britons were so astonished **that they stood
    motionless**.*

3   tantī erant clāmōrēs Modestī ut tōta castra
    complērent.
    *So great were the shouts of Modestus **that they
    filled the whole camp**.*

4   tantus erat numerus mīlitum ut Britannōs
    facile superārent.
    *So great was the number of the soldiers **that they
    easily overpowered the Britons**.*

Translations para. 2 p. 112

a   The boy was so stupid that everyone mocked him.

b   So great was the uproar that no one heard the orders of the centurions.

c   Agricola sent out so many soldiers that the enemy fled.

d   I feared my father so much that I did not dare to return home.

e   You had so many slaves that you could not count them.

f   Our slave-girls used to work so hard that we often praised them.

Table   SSB p. 87

Signal word	Meaning
tantus	*so great*
adeō	*so much*
tot	*so many*
tam	*so*

The legionary fortress SSB pp. 87–8

1

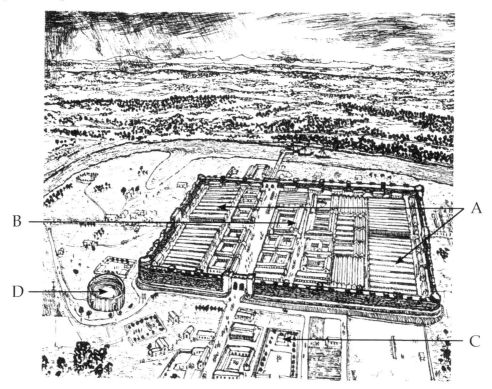

There are other barrack blocks where Modestus and Strythio might have lived besides those marked on this drawing. See the plan on p. 115.

2

	Latin word	Letter	Description
a	horreum	g	hospital
b	prīncipia	d	pair of rooms for eight men
c	sacellum	f	civilian settlement
d	contubernium	a	granary
e	praetōrium	b	headquarters building
f	vīcus	e	house of commanding officer
g	valētūdinārium	c	shrine

3 a The layout of legionary fortresses was standard.

   b Originally the number was 100.

   c Ovens at the edge of the fortress presented less of a fire-hazard.

   d The principia was the administrative heart of the fortress. It was safer to site it inside, not near the main gate, where it would be vulnerable to attack. It was the most impressive building in the fortress and contained the legion's chapel. It therefore occupied the most prominent and symbolic place in the fortress, at the junction of the two main roads, where it could be seen from the main gate.

Word patterns: adjectives and nouns   p. 113

2

adjectives		nouns	
sōlus	*alone, lonely*	solitūdō	*loneliness*
magnus	*large*	magnitūdō	*largeness, great size*
lātus	*wide*	lātitūdō	*width*
mānsuētus	*tame*	mānsuētūdō	*tameness*

3 fortitūdō *bravery*; pulchritūdō *beauty*; multitūdō *crowd*.

4 *longitude, solicitude, altitude* (**altus** can also mean *high*), *solitude, magnitude, latitude, fortitude, pulchritude* (a rare word), *multitude*.

Practising the language

Paras 1–3   p. 114

1 a The workman, standing near the door of the shop, was watching the fight.

   b Vilbia, having come out of the kitchen, immediately searched for her sister.

   c The thieves, (having been) led to the judge, asked for mercy/pardon.

   d The centurion, having obtained a jar of excellent wine, quickly returned to his friends.

   e Suddenly we heard horses approaching.

   f The clever boy found the money (which had been) hidden in the ground.

Participle	Description	Noun
a stāns	present	faber
b ēgressa	perfect active	Vilbia
c ductī	perfect passive	fūrēs
d adeptus	perfect active	centuriō
e appropinquantēs	present	equōs
f cēlātam	perfect passive	pecūniam

2 a Imperātor **īnsulās** vīsitābat.
      The emperor was visiting the islands.

   b **nautae** pecūniam **poscēbant**.
      The sailors were demanding money.

   c haec verba **senēs** terrēbant.
      These words terrified the old men.

   d iuvenēs **captīvōs** custōdiēbant.
      The young men were guarding the prisoners.

   e fūr **pōcula** īnspiciēbat.
      The thief was inspecting the wine-cups.

   f **leōnēs** ad pāstōrem **contendēbant**.
      The lions were hurrying towards the shepherd.

   g equī **flūmina** trānsīre nōlēbant.
      The horses did not want to cross the rivers.

   h **templa** in forō **erant**.
      The temples were in the forum.

3 a puella tabernam meam intrāvit. puell**ae** multōs ānulōs ostendī.
      The girl entered my shop. I showed many rings to the girl.

   b puer**ī** per viam currēbant. clāmōrēs puer**ōrum** mē excitāvērunt.
      The boys were running through the street. The shouts of the boys woke me.

   c Salvius ad aulam rēg**is** quam celerrimē contendit.
      Salvius hurried as quickly as possible to the palace of the king.

   d serv**ī** prope iānuam stābant. serv**īs** pecūniam dedimus.
      The slaves were standing near the door. We gave money to the slaves.

e Memor, ubi nōmen tuum audīvit,
perterritus erat.
*Memor, when he heard your name, was
terrified.*

f in hāc viā sunt duo templa.
In this road there are two temples.

g mercātor ad fundum meum heri vēnit.
frūmentum meum mercātōrī vēndidī.
*The merchant came to my farm yesterday. I
sold my grain to the merchant.*

h magna multitūdō cīvium nōbīs obstābat.
*A large crowd of citizens was standing in our
way.*

i barbarī prōvinciam oppugnāvērunt,
multāsque urbēs dēlēvērunt.
*Barbarians attacked the province, and they
destroyed many cities.*

j iūdex mercātōrem, quī fēminam
dēcēperat, pūnīvit.
*The judge punished the merchant, who had
deceived the woman.*

Further work SSB p. 89
manus mīlitum
*a band **of soldiers***
Nigrīna, optima saltātrīcum
*Nigrina, the best **of dancing-girls***
magnus numerus nāvium
*a great number **of ships***

Vocabulary checklist 27 SSB p. 89

1 An *apparent* reason appears real, rather than
actually being real.

2 *Arson* is the crime of deliberately setting fire
to something, especially a building (from
ardēre *to be on fire*).

3 An *imperious* tone is domineering, bossy,
commanding.

4 An *incendiary* bomb is designed to set fire to
things (from **incendere** *to set on fire*).

5 An *insidious* disease is unpleasant because it
develops unnoticed, without causing alarm.
The connection with **īnsidiae** is because it is
like an ambush, secret and deadly.

6 A *manual* could also be called a **hand**book
(from **manus**).

7 The shopping-centre's *proximity* to bus and
train routes refers to its nearness to them.

8 The *quality* of the essay refers to what sort
of essay it is, how good it is, rather than how
big it is.

9 No. *Sub*-standard is below standard.

10 A *tacit* agreement is unspoken, silent.

Language test SSB pp. 89–90

1 **a** Agricola, greatly alarmed, gave an order
to the commander/legatus.
iussum: accusative singular

b A huge crowd of citizens surrounded the
senator in the forum.
cīvium: genitive plural

c The reward which Modestus had
received did not please him.
praemium: nominative singular

d Quintus and Dumnorix caught sight
of a large band of horsemen/cavalry
approaching.
manum: accusative singular; **equitum**:
genitive plural

2 **a** fēmina mīlitem ōrāvit **ut fīlium servāret**.
The woman begged the soldier to save her son.

b mercātor tot gemmās habēbat **ut eās
numerāre nōn posset**.
*The merchant had so many jewels that he
could not count them.*

c puerī adeō timēbant **ut respondēre nōn
audērent**.
*The boys were so afraid that they dared not
answer.*

d pater meus saepe mē monēbat **ut ante
noctem domum redīrem**.
*My father often used to advise me to return
home before nightfall.*

e tantum erat perīculum **ut dē vītā
dēspērārēmus**.
*The danger was so great that we despaired of
our lives.*

f centuriō vōbīs imperāvit **ut ad prīncipia
contenderētis**.
*The centurion commanded you to hurry to the
headquarters.*

3   a   ēheu! domus tua **ardet**!

Oh no! Your house is on fire!

ardet: 3rd person singular, present tense.

b   maximē **gaudēbam** quod dea precēs meās **audīverat**.

I rejoiced very much / I was extremely happy because the goddess had heard my prayers.

gaudēbam: 1st person singular, imperfect tense. **audīverat**: 3rd person singular, pluperfect tense.

c   cūr fīliīs adeō **nocuistī** ut tē vīsitāre **recūsārent**?

Why did you harm your sons so much that they refused to visit you?

nocuistī: 2nd person singular, perfect tense. **recūsārent**: 3rd person plural, imperfect subjunctive.

d   cum Modestus haec verba **dīxisset**, eī nōn **crēdidimus**.

When Modestus had said these words, we did not believe him.

dīxisset: 3rd person singular, pluperfect subjunctive. **crēdidimus**: 1st person plural, perfect tense.

Revision

Uses of the subjunctive   p. 163

1   a   When Agricola had inspected the legion, he praised the soldiers and centurions.

b   When the soothsayer was dining in the temple, the king himself was approaching.

2   a   I was uncertain how long the river was.

b   No one knew whether Modestus and Strythio had been soldiers in Africa.

c   The Romans did not know how many enemies remained in the camp.

d   He asked me whether my mother was living.

3   a   The friends hurried to the city to bring help to the citizens.

b   I wrote a letter to warn the commander about the danger.

Longer sentences   pp. 166–7

2   a   The centurion remained motionless.
The centurion remained motionless, although the enemy were approaching.
The centurion remained motionless, although the enemy, who were brandishing their spears, were approaching.

b   All the citizens applauded.
When the girls began to sing, all the citizens applauded.
When the girls, who were walking in front of the procession, began to sing, all the citizens applauded.

c   The messenger made for the headquarters.
The messenger who was carrying the letter made for the headquarters.
The messenger who was carrying the letter made for the headquarters, as soon as he arrived at the camp.

3   a   So great were the flames that they were destroying the large house which a famous architect had built.

b   The freedman did not want to enter the bedroom because Modestus, who had drunk a lot of wine, was already deeply asleep.

c   Salvius, because he distrusted (*lit.* having distrusted) Belimicus, summoned a tribune to find out the truth.

d   After we came to the forum, where the merchants were accustomed to do their business, we saw a marvellous thing.

e   When the father saw his sons draining the cups, he was extremely furious.

f   Agricola soon found out where the enemy had placed their camp, how many soldiers there were in the camp, (and) whether they had horses.

Stage 28 imperium

Model sentences

Translation pp. 122–4

After the death of Cogidubnus, Salvius took over his kingdom. Immediately he began to extort money from the Britons. Belimicus, the chieftain of the Cantici, was helping Salvius.

Near the palace lived a British farmer who refused to hand over money to Salvius. So Salvius ordered the soldiers to ransack the farmer's small house/cottage. He put a centurion in charge of the soldiers.

1 The soldiers, armed with swords and spears, attacked the farmer's cottage.
2 The farmer, wounded by the centurion's sword, fell down unconscious.
3 The slaves fled, frightened by the shouts.
4 The farmer's son, armed with a club, resisted in vain.
5 Belimicus, encouraged by hope of a reward, was helping and urging on the Roman soldiers.
6 Then the soldiers entered the cottage and carried out a chest filled with money.
7 Then the soldiers led the women, bound in chains, to the camp.
8 Finally the soldiers set fire to the cottage. The flames, increased by the wind, quickly consumed the cottage.
9 Shepherds, who lived near the cottage, were standing motionless, astonished by the sight.
    They saw the cottage, consumed by the flames.
    They saw the farmer's son, seriously wounded by a spear.
    They saw the farmer himself, killed by the centurion's sword.
    Finally they went away, moved by anger, cursing Belimicus and the Romans.

Questions SSB pp. 92–3

1 He took over Cogidubnus' kingdom. He at once began to extort money from the Britons.
2 A British farmer, living near the palace, refused to hand over money.

3 He ordered the soldiers to ransack the farmer's small house/cottage.
4 a Belimicus, chieftain of the Cantici, was helping Salvius.
   b He put a centurion in command of the soldiers.

Sentence 1
a They attacked the farmer's cottage.
b With swords and spears.

Sentence 2
The farmer, wounded **by the sword** of the centurion, fell down unconscious.

Sentence 3
Frightened by the shouts.

Sentence 4
With a club. One young boy and a club was of no use against several soldiers with swords and spears.

Sentence 5
(Having been) led on by hope of a reward.

Sentence 6
The chest was filled with money.

Sentence 7
Then the soldiers led the women, **bound in chains**, to the camp.

Sentences 8
The flames, **increased by the wind**, quickly consumed the cottage.

Sentences 9
Shepherds, who lived near the cottage, were standing motionless, astonished by the sight.
    They saw the cottage, consumed by the flames.
    They saw the farmer's son, seriously wounded by a spear.
    They saw the farmer himself, killed by the centurion's sword.
    Finally they went away, moved by anger, cursing Belimicus and the Romans.

testāmentum

Questions SSB pp. 93–4

1   morbō gravī afflīctus.
     *Afflicted by a severe illness / when he was gravely
     ill.*

2   The Emperor Domitian (Titus Flavius
     Domitianus). His kingdom and the citizens of
     the Regnenses.

3   To obey the laws and to lead a quiet life.

4

Beneficiary	Bequest	Reason for bequest
Cn. Iūlius Agricola	Cogidubnus' statue made by a British craftsman.	Agricola can keep Cogidubnus in mind through his whole life.
C. Salvius Līberālis	Two silver tripods.	Salvius is the most loyal of Cogidubnus' friends and is a very shrewd man.
L. Marcius Memor	Cogidubnus' villa near Aquae Sulis.	Memor welcomed Cogidubnus kindly when he came to the baths seeking help from the goddess Sulis.
Dumnorix	One thousand gold pieces and Cogidubnus' palace.	Cogidubnus loved Dumnorix like a son.
Belimicus	Five hundred gold pieces and a very fast ship.	Belimicus saved Cogidubnus from a bear raging through his palace.

5   Salvius. He wants to make sure that he has
     a proper burial, and that all his dearest
     possessions are with him in the next world.

6   His jewels, gold bowls, and all the weapons
     he has acquired for war and for hunting.
     Archaeologists often find examples of 'grave
     goods' such as pottery bowls and jewellery.
     Rich burials like that of Cogidubnus are
     found, but they are of course much rarer.

7   Cogidubnus is establishing that the will is
     genuine, not forged.

8   It is surprising that Salvius, Cogidubnus'
     enemy, is referred to as the most loyal
     of his friends, admired by the king for
     his shrewdness and now left the dead
     Dumnorix's share of the will. Memor, who
     plotted to poison the king, is thanked for his
     kindness to him and rewarded with a villa.
     Belimicus, a supporter of Salvius against
     Cogidubnus, is rewarded for saving the
     king's life; this is a false statement, as the
     rescuer was Quintus. Salvius seems likely to
     benefit greatly from the will. Explanations for
     this could be:

     a   the will was made some time before
          Cogidubnus was betrayed by the
          Romans;

     b   the will was a forgery;

     c   Cogidubnus was a very ill old man and
          confused.

Picture question   p. 125

The building is Cogidubnus' palace at Fishbourne.
Salvius' portrait has been superimposed because
he is the new owner.

in aulā Salviī

Questions p. 127

Marks

1 Salvius was in the camp / at Chester. He travelled to the palace. 2

2 Nine days. He stayed to look after the affairs of Cogidubnus. 2

3 He began to extort money and property from the Britons. 1

4 Greed and fear. 1

5 He received many rewards and honours from Salvius. He wanted to become king of the Regnenses. 2

6 The chieftains told him. 1

7 Salvius decided to kill Belimicus. He asked his friends whether he should use violence or poison. 2

8 The friend suggested poison was most suitable. There was a problem with administering it since Belimicus trusted no one. 2

9 *Two of:* The friend said it was easy to deceive Belimicus; mixing poison with food had already deceived cleverer men than Belimicus; the friend himself knew how to administer the poison in an expert manner. 2

10 It would be very easy to invite Belimicus to a lavish dinner. 1

11 He would send Belimicus a flattering letter. Belimicus could not resist soft and flattering words / flattery. 2

12 *either:* **epistulā mendācī dēceptus**
       deceived by the lying letter;
    or: **neque ūllam fraudem suspicātus**
       and not having suspected any trick;
    or: **ad aulam nōnā hōrā vēnit.** *He came to the palace at the ninth hour.*
    One mark for Latin, one mark for translation. 2

TOTAL 20

Further work SSB p. 95

1 a *Some chieftains, corrupted by greed and fear.* The chieftains' actions were motivated by greed. They probably expected a reward from Salvius. They were also frightened of him and wanted to keep his favour. Salvius appears to command obedience by being tyrannical and using bribery.

  b *(Belimicus), led on by this hope.* He hoped to become king of the Regnenses.

  c *Salvius, angered by Belimicus' audacity.* Belimicus had received many rewards and honours from Salvius, but was still not satisfied.

  d *Poison mixed with food.* One of Salvius' friends.

  e *Salvius, delighted by his friend's plan.* Salvius will not have to take any risks himself. His friend is sure of success and knows how to administer the poison himself.

  f *He (Belimicus), deceived by the lying letter.* An invitation to a lavish dinner at the palace, written in words that were flattering and irresistible to Belimicus.

2 a Belimicus began to conspire with a few chieftains. However, *they / the chieftains* reported the plot to Salvius.

  b Salvius invited Belimicus to the palace. *He/Belimicus* came to the palace at the ninth hour.

The words above *in italics* are better translations than *who*.

Further examples p. 155

2 a 'Why do you give me nothing?' asked the son. When he had heard *this*, his father was very angry.

  b The merchant handed over the money to the slave-girls. After they counted the denarii, *they / the slave-girls* returned to the house.

  c Then the king gave Memor a sign. Wearing a splendid toga, *he/Memor* advanced solemnly to the altar.

  d Many soldiers were now filling the palace. When they had seen *them*, the priests got up.

About the language 1: the ablative case   p. 128   SSB pp. 95–6

1   *By* or *with.*

3   a   Astonished by Belimicus' boldness, Salvius said nothing.
        audāciā: singular.

    b   The merchant, beaten with clubs, was lying unconscious in the ditch.
        fūstibus: plural.

    c   Defended by a wall, the soldiers resisted the barbarians for a long time.
        mūrō: singular.

    d   My wife bought a ring, decorated with jewels.
        gemmīs: plural.

    e   The guests, delighted by the slave-girl's skill, applauded.
        arte: singular.

Further work

	nominative singular	*ablative singular*	*ablative plural*
first declension	**iniūria**	iniūriā	**iniūriīs**
	catēna	**catēnā**	catēnīs
second declension	**gladius**	gladiō	**gladiīs**
third declension	**clāmor**	**clāmōre**	clāmōribus

cēna Salviī

Translation lines 1–11   p. 129   SSB p. 96

Salvius received Belimicus kindly **as he entered the palace** and led him into the dining-room. There **they dined alone** lavishly and in high spirits. Belimicus, **having caught sight of Salvius smiling** and relaxed by the wine, **began to speak** boldly:

'My dear Salvius, **you have received** many great acts of kindness from me. After **Quintus and Dumnorix escaped**; I alone helped you; having pursued them **for many days on end, I killed Dumnorix; I told** many lies **to Agricola in order to condemn** Cogidubnus for treachery. For such great favours as these **I ask for** a well-deserved reward.'

When he heard this, Salvius was **inflamed by Belimicus' arrogance**, but concealed his anger and answered **courteously**.

Questions   SSB pp. 96–7

1   He tells Belimicus that he has already prepared a well-deserved reward for him.

2   He asks Belimicus why he is not eating anything and says he wants him to taste a very special sauce that he has imported from Spain. He orders a boy to bring it for them both.

3   No. The slave gave the same to Salvius as well as to Belimicus.

4   He asked what Belimicus was claiming in return for the great services he had done for him.

5   Belimicus said that he was not satisfied with the five hundred gold coins which he had received from Cogidubnus' will and that he claimed the kingdom itself.

    Salvius might be surprised that Belimicus was so outspoken but would be expecting this reply, as the chieftains had told him of Belimicus' plot.

6   Salvius said that he, not Cogidubnus, had given them to Belimicus.

7   He knows that, if his plan works, Belimicus will soon be dead and not able to betray him. Belimicus' reaction will probably be a mixture of horror, disbelief, anger and frustration.

8   The boy slave has just come in with the special sauce as ordered by Salvius (line 14).

Further work   SSB p. 97

Words like **benignē** *kindly* and **audācter** *boldly* are called adverbs.

About the language 2: expressions of time   p. 130   SSB p. 97

3   a   The guests were dining for three hours.
        trēs hōrās: accusative

    b   On the fourth day the king returned.
        quārtō diē: ablative

    c   Agricola governed the province for seven years.
        septem annōs: accusative

d At the second hour the freedman tried to wake up Memor.

secundā hōrā: ablative

e The enemy attacked our camp in the middle of the night.

mediā nocte: ablative

f We were sailing for six days; on the seventh day we arrived at the harbour.

sex diēs: accusative

septimō diē: ablative

Picture question SSB p. 97

Garum is a fish sauce.

Belimicus rēx

Questions lines 1–11 SSB pp. 97–8

1 He had just learnt that Salvius had forged Cogidubnus' will. He was so astonished that he could not give any reply.

2 Salvius was probably laughing with pleasure at the shock he had given Belimicus and because he knew that there was worse to come for him. His plan seemed to be working well.

According to Salvius, Belimicus and Cogidubnus were always enemies, so he should not have expected anything from the king's will.

3 He said that they were friends.

4 **a** He would begin to be pleased when Salvius said that he was greatly in his debt.

b At the mention of Salvius' intention to make him a king, he would be more pleased, happily assuming that he was about to get what he wanted, the kingdom of the Regnenses.

c When Salvius said that his intended kingdom for Belimicus was much larger than that of Cogidubnus, he would be unbelievably overjoyed.

5 Salvius was cunning enough to call for more sauce while Belimicus' attention was fully on his intended kingdom. Salvius gave his order to the slave who went out immediately, returned with the poisoned sauce and poured it into Belimicus' bowl only.

6 He was so overjoyed at the thought of his reward that he was completely off his guard. He had also previously tasted the sauce without any ill effect.

Translation lines 12–21 p. 131 SSB p. 98

Belimicus: How big is this kingdom which you have promised me? Where in the world is it?

Salvius: *(laughing loudly)* **It is much greater than the Roman empire.**

Belimicus: *(alarmed by these words)* You have drunk too much, my friend. I know of no kingdom greater than the Roman empire.

Salvius: **It is the kingdom to where all men depart in the end. It is the kingdom from where no one can return. Belimicus, I make you king of the dead.**

Filming notes lines 22–end SSB pp. 98–9

Belimicus (lines 22–6)

State of mind: Very frightened and very angry.

Physical symptoms: Deathly pale, tongue-tied, ears ringing, painful stomach cramps.

Tone of speech: Defiant, challenging, threatening.

Salvius (lines 27–9)

Appearance: Calm, unafraid of Belimicus' threats.

Tone of speech: Confident, triumphant, mocking.

Death of Belimicus (lines 30–1)

Racked with pain from the poison; gives final loud groan and drops dead.

Disposal of body (lines 31–3)

Change of tempo: In contrast to previous tension of the administering and working of the poison, now swift action.

Cremation: Slaves appear immediately and drag body out into garden (assume pyre already set up). Helped by favourable wind, flames very quickly consume body.

End of scene (**sīc Salvius … manērent** *lines 33–4*)

How to convey visually / with speech. Two ideas:

1 Salvius summons two or three chieftains to him. They see the pyre burning in the background and get the message. No speech necessary.

2 Salvius is seen entertaining chieftains to dinner. There is one empty place. Salvius says '**Belimicus iam abiit. vōbīs grātiās agō quod vōs in fidē manētis.**'

You may have other good ideas.

About the language 3: prepositions

Para. 4 p. 132

a Two friends were making a journey to the city.

b Near the goddess' temple was a sacred spring.

c The chieftains were having a conversation about Belimicus' death.

d In front of the palace were standing four guards.

e The centurion returned without the soldiers.

f The sailor steered the ship around the rock.

g There was a deep river between the Romans and the enemy.

h Modestus did not want to fight against the barbarians.

Further work   SSB pp. 99–100

List of prepositions

Accusative	Translation
ad urbem	to the city
prope templum	near the temple
circum saxum	around the rock
inter Rōmānōs et hostēs	between the Romans and the enemy
contrā barbarōs	against the barbarians
ante bellum	before the war
trāns flūmen	across the river
extrā mūrōs	outside the walls
post cēnam	after dinner
per hostēs	through the enemy
in tabernam	into the pub/shop
in mēnsam	onto the table

Ablative	Translation
dē morte	about the death
prō aulā	in front of the palace
sine mīlitibus	without the soldiers
ā silvā	from the wood
cum amīcīs	with the friends
ē fonte	out of the fountain
in castrīs	in the camp
in monte	on the mountain

Para. 5 p. 133

a The slave-girl took the centurion into the pub/shop.

b The dog jumped onto the table.

c The soldiers were working in the camp.

d There was a splendid temple on the mountain.

Interpreting the evidence: our knowledge of Roman Britain

SSB pp. 100–2

Literary evidence

1 Satisfaction that their efforts have been appreciated and acknowledged; pride in their achievements; respect for their commander, Agricola; confidence that they would win the battle; relief at a possible end to the present campaign; a strong feeling of patriotism; contempt for the enemy.

2 *Romans sympathetic to Agricola* would feel pride in Rome's successes and the enlargement of the empire; respect and admiration for Agricola's qualities.

   Romans unsympathetic to Agricola might feel jealousy, suspicion about the accuracy of the speech and cynicism at the rhetoric.

3 From talking with his father-in-law, Agricola; from soldiers who were there at the time; from other written evidence. Some, if not all, of the speech may have been invented by Tacitus. This would have been acceptable at the time.

4 He wanted the speech to illustrate Agricola's character and military prowess and so enhance his father-in-law's reputation. Inserting speeches also enlivens a narrative and was a common practice among classical writers.

Archaeological evidence

1 In a rescue excavation the archaeologists have a limited time to 'rescue' the evidence that the site contains. They try to excavate and record as much as possible before the contractors destroy or rebury the site.

2 In order to reach the lower layers of a site, the upper layers are inevitably destroyed. Therefore each layer must be slowly and carefully examined. It has to be recorded by photographs, drawings, notes, etc., as the different layers contain evidence from the various times that the site was used. Evidence is derived from any foundations and their position, from different coloured earth, styles of pottery, dates of coins and other remains.

3 The picture on the left shows the earlier excavation. The picture on the right recalls the lines of holes found at Fishbourne. These were probably for poles to support a trellis for climbing plants, such as roses (see Stage 16, pp. 72–3).

4 **a** An antefix tile from a roof in Chester. It would inform archaeologists that there had been a building there and, from the inscription and wild boar device, that the Twentieth Legion had been operating there. This would help to date the building.

   b A section of a mosaic floor from Fishbourne. This would give archaeologists information about the type of material used and its source, whether local or imported, the style of the design, the probable nationality of the craftsmen, a possible dating, the kind of owner of the building from which it came.

   c Slave neck-chain from East Anglia. Archaeologists would learn that slaves were used at that site, which was probably on a large estate. They would be interested in the material and design, in comparison with others found elsewhere.

5

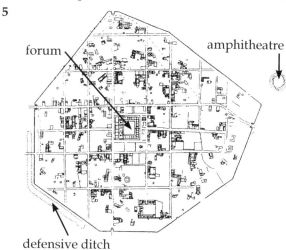

forum   amphitheatre

defensive ditch

6 Nearly all the streets are laid out in a grid system. This was also seen in Pompeii (see Stage 3, p. 34) and Alexandria (see Stage 17, pp. 84–5).

7

London	Londinium
Bath	Aquae Sulis
Chester	Deva
Silchester	Calleva
Chichester	Noviomagus
York	Eboracum
Gloucester	Glevum
Colchester	Camulodunum
St Albans	Verulamium
Carlisle	Luguvalium
Corbridge	Corstopitum
Caerleon	Isca
Wroxeter	Viroconium
Exeter	Isca
Lincoln	Lindum
Cirencester	Corinium

8 Town names derived from **castra**:

-chester: Manchester, Winchester, Rochester, Dorchester.

Caer-: Caernarvon, Caerphilly.

-cester: Towcester, Gloucester, Leicester.

-caster: Doncaster, Lancaster.

You may be able to think of other examples.

Word patterns: adjectives and nouns

Paras. 2 and 3 p. 133

2   superbus   *proud*
    superbia   **pride**
    trīstis   **sad**
    trīstitia   **sadness**
    perītus   **skilful, experienced**
    perītia   *skill, experience*
    prūdēns   *shrewd, sensible*
    prūdentia   **shrewdness, common sense**
    sapiēns   **wise**
    sapientia **wisdom**
    ēlegāns   **elegant**
    ēlegantia   **elegance**

3   boldness, friendship, arrogance, power, treachery.

Question SSB p. 103

All the nouns are *abstract* nouns. They are expressing someone's feelings or attributes.

Practising the language

Exercise 1 p. 134

a   Quīntus nesciēbat quō modō Cogidubnus periisse**t**.
    Quintus did not know how Cogidubnus had died.

b   cīvēs, cum tabernam intrāvisse**nt**, vīnum poposcērunt.
    When the citizens had entered the inn, they asked for wine.

c   Agricola mīlitibus imperāvit ut ad castra redīre**nt**.
    Agricola ordered the soldiers to return to the camp.

d   tantus erat clāmor ut nēmō centuriōnem audīre**t**.
    So great was the noise that no one heard the centurion.

e   nōs, cum Agricolam vīdissē**mus**, maximē gaudēbāmus.
    When we had seen Agricola, we were extremely pleased.

f   rēxne tibi persuāsit ut sēcum templum vīsitārē**s**?
    Did the king persuade you to visit the temple with him?

g   domum rediī ut parentēs meōs adiuvāre**m**.
    I returned home in order to help my parents.

h   cūr dīcere nōlēbātis ubi illō diē mātrem vestram vīdissē**tis**?
    Why did you not want to say where you had seen your mother that day?

Further work SSB p. 103
Reasons for the use of the subjunctive:

a   indirect question
b   after **cum**
c   indirect command
d   result clause
e   after **cum**
f   indirect command
g   purpose clause
h   indirect question

Exercise 2 p. 134

a   nūntius, **gladiō** graviter vulnerātus, effugere nōn poterat.
    The messenger, badly wounded by a sword, wasn't able to get away.

b   Salvius, **audāciā** eius attonitus, diū tacēbat.
    Astounded by his boldness, Salvius was silent for some time.

c   captīvī, **catēnīs** vīnctī, in longīs ōrdinibus stābant.
    The prisoners, bound in chains, were standing in long rows.

d   Britannī, **fūstibus** armātī, pugnāre volēbant.
    Armed with clubs, the Britons were willing to fight.

e   dominus, **īrā** commōtus, omnēs servōs carnificibus trādidit.
    The master, shaken with anger, handed over all the slaves to the executioners.

f   hospitēs, **vīnō** solūtī, clāmāre et iocōs facere coepērunt.
    Relaxed by the wine, the guests began to shout and make jokes.

Interpreting the evidence

continued

Inscriptional evidence   pp. 140–1

First inscription

1   Caecilius Avitus.
2   optio.
3   The Twentieth Legion Valeria Victrix.
4   34 years.
5   15 years.

The full inscription would read:

    D(IS) M(ANIBUS)
    CAECILIUS AVIT
    US EMER(ITA) AUG(USTA)
    OPTIO LEG(IONIS) XX
    V(ALERIAE) V(ICTRICIS)
    ST(I)P(ENDIORUM)
    XV VIX(IT)
    AN(NOS) XXXIIII
    H(ERES) F(ACIENDUM) C(URAVIT)

Emerita Augusta, a Roman colony in Spain (now Merida), would have been the birthplace of Caecilius Avitus.

Second inscription

The soldier's name: Caius (or Gaius) Lovesius Cadarus.

His voting tribe: the Papirian tribe.

His birthplace: Emerita Augusta (like Caecilius Avitus above).

His rank: private soldier.

His legion: the Twentieth Legion Valeria Victrix.

His age: 25 years.

His length of service: 8 years. Note that 8 is shown as IIX rather than VIII.

His heir, Frontinius Aquilo, had the stone set up.

The full inscription would read:

    C(AIUS) LOVESIUS PAPIR(IA TRIBU)
    CADARUS EMERITA MIL(ES)
    LEG(IONIS) XX V(ALERIAE) V(ICTRICIS)
    AN(NORUM) XXV STIP(ENDIORUM) IIX
    FRONTINIUS AQUILO H(ERES)
    F(ACIENDUM) C(URAVIT)

Note that the optio was 19 years old when he joined the legion, while the soldier was only 17 years old.

Vocabulary checklist 28

SSB pp. 103–4

1   The dancers in a *corps de ballet* must be slim and physically fit. *Corpulent* people are overweight. A corps is a body or group of people; corpulent means big-bodied. Both words come from **corpus** *body*.

2   An *irascible* person is inclined or quick to become angry. Someone who is *irate* is actually being angry (from **īra** *anger*).

3   The defendant was accused of planning his evil deed before he actually committed it. The word *malice* is derived from **malus** *evil* or *bad*.

4   In furnishing his home in an *opulent* style, the owner wanted to convey an impression of riches and wealth (from **opēs**).

5   **spēs** means *hope*, **spērāre** *to hope*, and **dēspērāre** *to give up hope* or *to despair*.

6   **ut vīdī** *as I saw*; **ut flōrēs vidērem** *in order that I might see the flowers*.

7   A *ventilator* lets in air (from **ventus** *wind*).

8   To decide; you were in pain; I had entrusted; they (have) killed.

Numbers

1   A cycle with *one* wheel; a musical performance by *two* singers or instrumentalists; a *three*-pronged spear; a *four*-line verse; a Roman ship with *five* banks of oars on each side; a group of *six* people, usually singers or instrumentalists; a person in his or her *seventies*; a series of *eight* notes; the *ninth* month in the Roman year; a system of calculating based on the number *ten*.

2   They all end in -**ginta**.

3   A centilitre.

Language test   SSB p. 104

1   a   sex annōs
     b   septem diēs
     c   prīmō diē
     d   illā nocte
     e   secundō annō
     f   quattuor noctēs
     g   quīnque hōrās
     h   tertiā hōrā

2 a The Britons, inflamed *with anger*, resisted the Romans bravely. ablative: **īrā**.

b The boy, killed *by the swords* of the soldiers, was lying in front of the cottage. ablative: **gladiīs**.

c The soldiers drew up the women, moved *by fear*, into a line. ablative: **metū**.

d Some chieftains, led on *by hope* of a reward, decided to help Salvius. ablative: **spē**.

e Salvius kindly received Belimicus, deceived *by the letter* and having suspected nothing. ablative: **epistulā**.

f The Britons, warned *by the death* of Belimicus, never afterwards tried to plot against Salvius. ablative: **morte**.

Revision

Uses of the cases   SSB p. 105

1 Check your translations with the ones in *italic type* on the right of p. 160.

2 a Modestus was a man of very little intelligence. **prūdentiae**: genitive.

b I lived there for many years. **annōs**: accusative.

c Why did you not believe me? **mihi**: dative.

d Have you drunk enough wine? **vīnī**: genitive.

e The chieftain recalled the names of the young men. **nōmina**: accusative; **iuvenum**: genitive.

f The old man told us the story about Caesar's death. **morte**: ablative.

g We departed at the seventh hour. **hōrā**: ablative.

h Belimicus, deceived by Salvius' words, agreed. **verbīs**: ablative; **Salviī**: genitive.

Uses of the subjunctive   p. 164

4 a The messenger persuaded the Britons to bring gifts to the palace.

b The old man begged the goddess Sulis to cure his illness.

5 a I guarded the prison so carefully that the commander himself praised me.

b The merchant had so many statues that he could not count them.

7 a When he had drunk the poison, the freedman fell down dead.

b So many enemies were attacking our camp that we were in despair for our lives.

c The chieftains asked me why I wanted to cross the bridge.

d Gutta hid under the table to / in order to avoid the danger.

e The centurions ordered the soldiers to repair the granaries.

f When the slave-girls were washing the wine-cups, four horsemen arrived at the pub.

g My son was so astonished that he stood motionless for a long time.

h We opened the doors of the cells in order to set free our friends.

i My friend warned me to lie hidden.

j Modestus was not able to explain how the prisoners had escaped.

Reasons for subjunctive

a used with **cum**

b result clause

c indirect question

d purpose clause

e indirect command

f used with **cum**

g result clause

h purpose clause

i indirect command

j indirect question

General vocabulary practice

SSB pp. 105–6

1 Odd one out:

a **comes** *companion*. The rest are parts of the body.

b **Mārs** the god of war. The rest are goddesses.

c **prīnceps** *chieftain*. The rest are ranks in the Roman army.

d **nāvis** *ship*. The rest are people in certain occupations.

e **scelestus** *wicked*. The rest are good qualities.

f **tacēre** *to be quiet*. The rest express sound of some kind.

g **nox** *night*. The rest are all negative words.

h **nōmen** *name*. The rest express some aspect of time.

i **novem** *nine*. The rest are all even numbers.

j **tuus** *your*: adjective. The rest are pronouns.

2 Words of opposite meaning:

	Word	Letter	Opposite word
a	benignus	e	perfidus
b	ingressus	f	mors
c	velle	a	crūdēlis
d	mortuus	g	inimīcus
e	fidēlis	l	paucī
f	vīta	h	taceō
g	amīcus	b	ēgressus
h	clāmō	c	nōlle
i	aperiō	j	dēleō
j	aedificō	d	vīvus
k	terra	k	mare
l	multī	i	claudō

3 Words in order of magnitude:

a	domus	oppidum	urbs
b	īnfāns	puer	vir
c	arānea	canis	equus
d	quadrāgintā	septuāgintā	nōnāgintā
e	magnus	maior	maximus
f	diēs	mēnsis	annus
g	mīles	cohors	legiō
h	pugiō	gladius	hasta
i	dēns	oculus	genū
j	fōns	flūmen	mare